Glimpsing the Face of God

Glimpsing the Face of God

The Search for Meaning in the Universe

Alister McGrath

A LION BOOK

Published by
Lion Publishing plc
Mayfield House, 256 Banbury Road,
Oxford OX2 7DH, England
www.lion-publishing.co.uk
ISBN 0 7459 5026 4

First edition 2002
10 9 8 7 6 5 4 3 2 1 0

Text acknowledgments
p. 10: extract from 'High Flight' by John Gillespie Magee, published in *More Poems from the Forces: A Collection of Verses by Serving Members of the Navy, Army and Air Force* by Keidrich Rhys, London: George Routledge and Sons, 1943.
pp. 57, 66, 68, 81, 84, 113: the scripture quotations contained herein are from The Revised Standard Version of the Bible, copyright © 1946, 1952, 1971 by the Division of Christian Education of the National Council of the Churches of Christ in the United States of America, and are used by permission. All rights reserved.
p. 116: extract from 'Prayer to Christ' by Anselm of Canterbury, published in *The Prayers and Meditations of St Anselm*, translated by Benedicta Ward, Penguin Classics, 1973. Copyright © Benedicta Ward. Reproduced by permission of Penguin Books Ltd.

A catalogue record for this book is available
from the British Library

Typeset in 10/15 Berkeley Oldstyle
Printed and bound in Singapore

Contents

1 Intimations of a Beyond

Since history began, people have been enthralled by the wonder of the sky at night. Few have failed to be overwhelmed by the solemn stillness of the star-studded heavens. The great astronomers of ancient Assyria and Babylon traced the slow movement of the planets through the heavens, wondering if they might somehow shape the mystery of human destiny. The ancient Greeks saw patterns in the stars, and named these constellations after their heroes – Orion the great hunter, Pegasus the flying horse and Andromeda the doomed heroine.

As time went on, the spectacle of the night sky proved to be useful, as well as dramatic. The ancient Egyptians learned to predict the annual flooding of the Nile – of such central importance to the nation's agriculture – by watching for the rising of the star we know as Sirius. The Arabs developed the astrolabe as a way of determining the position of a ship with reference to the stars, allowing mariners to plot their course across the oceans.

Yet not all experienced a sense of wonder when contemplating the starlit heavens. For some, the lonely pinpoints of light against the dark velvet of the night speak of loneliness and pointlessness. Those same stars have witnessed generations rising and falling. Human empires rise and fall; the same stars shone down on them all. The same stars shone while generation after generation flourished, and passed into the dust. Like Tennyson's 'The Brook', they remind us of the brevity of human life:

> For men may come and men may go,
> but I go on for ever.

The heavens thus heighten our sense of transience, forcing us to ask whether this life is all that we can hope for. Is there more to life than we know? And can the silent witness of those distant stars help us to find it?

The *Rubáiyát of Omar Khayyám*, one of the finest works of Persian literature, also gives expression to the deep sense of despondency evoked by the heavens. We are powerless to change our destiny. The sun, moon and stars declare both our transience and apparent inability to change our situation:

And that inverted Bowl we call 'the Sky',
  whereunder crawling coop'd we live and die,
lift not thy hands to It for help – for It
  rolls impotently on as Thou or I.

The stars can thus be a melancholy reminder of the vastness of the universe, and our utter insignificance within it. Perhaps the slowly orbiting planets are the secret masters of our destiny, influencing us in ways we could not even begin to understand, let alone to resist. The stars may evoke an unspeakable sense of yearning for something that seems unattainable – a sense of longing for something significant, which the night sky can heighten, yet not satisfy. Maybe the stars point to something mysterious, something unfathomable, which somehow lies beyond them. Something seems to lie beyond the whispering orbs of the night. But what? And how is it to be known?

Questions like these have intrigued people since the human race began to think. Maybe these are pointless questions, the musings of people who cannot cope with the sobering thought of mortality and meaninglessness. Yet perhaps we are meant to think such thoughts. Maybe the spectacle of the night sky is meant to trigger off such patterns of reflection within us – and, by doing so, open the door on a new way of thinking and living. We seem to have been created to ask questions – to try to make sense of what we see around us and how we fit into the greater scheme of things.

So what is it about human nature that makes it yearn to make sense of things? Why is it that the human mind seems able to gain access to at least something of the deep structuring of the universe, as the successes of the natural sciences remind us? It is almost as if the human mind was designed to discern the pattern of the universe and reflect on its meaning.

The French philosopher Blaise Pascal (1623–62) gave much thought of the relationship of the human mind to the vastness of the universe. In some respects, he noted, the human mind is totally overshadowed by the immensity of the universe. It seems so insignificant in comparison with the grandeur of the stars and planets. 'The eternal silence of these infinite spaces terrifies me,' he wrote. Yet, Pascal argued, in one sense the human mind was greater than all of these – precisely because it was able to know itself, as well as the stars. The human mind was able to take in the reality of the universe and reflect on its significance for its own meaning.

As we reflect on the wonder of the universe, we find questions being raised in our minds that both challenge and excite us. There seems to be some inbuilt longing for purpose which drives us to look for clues to the meaning of the universe. We contemplate the glory of the night sky, wondering if the silent beauty of the stars might cast light on the riddle of human destiny. Is our real homeland out there somewhere, beyond this world? We appreciate the beauty of a glorious sunset, while wondering if the sense of beauty it awakens within us is somehow a pointer to another and more wonderful world that we have yet to discover. Shelley put it like this in his 1824 poem 'To – One Word is Too Often Profaned':

> The desire of the moth for the star,
> of the night for the morrow,
> the devotion to something afar
> from the sphere of our sorrow.

We listen as a distinguished astronomer lectures on the remarkable ordering of the cosmos and wonder if this might lead us to discover the mind of God.

The Second World War pilot and poet John Gillespie Magee, Jr (1922–41) saw flying high above the earth as an image of a deeper journey:

> Oh! I have slipped the surly bonds of earth
> and danced the skies on laughter-silvered wings…
> put out my hand and touched the face of God.

Might our hopes and fears allow us to do the same? Or are we like the moth who feels drawn to the distant light of a star but has no hope of ever reaching this distant and lonely goal?

The importance of such issues has been recognized since the dawn of civilization. The earliest Greek philosophers – whom we refer to as the 'pre-Socratics' – argued endlessly about the nature of the world and how it came to be as it is. They insisted that the universe was rationally constructed and that it could therefore be understood through the right use of human reason and argument. Human beings had the ability to make sense of the universe. Socrates took this line of thought further, identifying a link between the way the universe was constructed and the best way for human beings to live. To reflect on the nature of the universe was to gain insights into the nature of the 'good life' – the best and most authentic way of living. Reflecting on the clues provided in the structuring of the world thus leads to an understanding of our identity and destiny.

SOCRATES

The same idea emerges in some of the writings of the Old Testament, especially those focusing on the theme of 'wisdom'. The wisdom writings of the Old Testament insisted that sense could be made of every aspect of life – from the movements of the stars to the behaviour of people. It was all a question of having the right explanatory framework. The wisdom writings credit Solomon, one of Israel's greatest kings, with immense insight in this respect. Observing the world opens the door to the understanding of the greater matters of life. The book of Job compares the human quest for wisdom to the mining of precious metals and stones from deep within the earth. They lie hidden from human view and must be sought out. Like the pearl of great price, true wisdom is profoundly worth seeking and possessing.

Deep down within us lies a relentless quest for meaning. Some might say that this is nothing more than a coping mechanism thrown up by the human mind to shield us from the unbearable pain of knowing that life is pointless. We dream of a universe in which we have meaning and purpose, and prefer to inhabit this imaginary country rather than face up to the bleak and grim barrenness of the real world.

Sigmund Freud (1856–1939) argued that talk about 'God' and such things was nothing more than a crude wish-fulfilment on the part of those who could not handle the harsh truth of a godless, meaningless universe. 'The interpretation of dreams', Freud wrote, 'is the royal road to a knowledge of the unconscious activities of the mind'. Imagine a young boy who longed for a racing cycle and expected his parents to give him one as a birthday present. On the great day, his well-meaning and sensible parents give him a set of advanced mathematical textbooks. The bicycle would live on in his dream world, as the boy imagined himself the proud possessor of the best racing bike imaginable. He would seek consolation in an imaginary world and close his mind to the disappointments of what he actually had been given. In the same way, Freud argued, all our thoughts and hopes of another world were nothing more than dreams and illusions, generated by our minds in a desperate attempt to mask the truth.

Karl Marx (1818–83) declared that our thoughts of God or a world beyond our present experience were just a way of coping with the harshness of our economic and social situation. Such thoughts consoled us in the sorrow and pain of life. They were the 'opium of the people', a narcotic that eased the pain of life and dulled our senses to the anguish of a meaningless world of suffering and oppression. Marx believed that a revolutionary change in both the social and economic systems would eliminate the sorrows of the world and make such thoughts utterly irrelevant. Yet people continued to dream and hope, even when Marx's brave new world was forcibly established in many parts of the world during the 20th century. The yearning went on. Something was missing.

Karl Marx

But what if these attempts to explain away our longing for meaning are misguided? What if we are meant to think such thoughts? What if the grandeur of the night sky was intended to trigger off a sense of longing within us, and heighten it? It is so easy to dismiss such reflections as invalid and illusory. Yet those who dismiss them often do so in pursuit of their own agendas. Marx sought consolation in his own illusion – that social revolution would achieve a human transformation and abolish any sense of longing. No longer is that illusion taken seriously. Marx was naturally obliged to rubbish alternative viewpoints in order to enhance the credibility of his own. But what if such thoughts are valid? What if the sense of longing and yearning that is evoked by the night sky is meant to lead us onwards on a voyage of discovery? What if nature is studded with clues to our true meaning and destiny, and fingerprinted with the presence of God? This book is an exploration of this fascinating possibility.

So where shall we begin? Perhaps the most obvious place is the human desire to make sense of our world, and what this implies.

2 Trying to Make Sense of Things

We long to make sense of things and often gain a sense of deep satisfaction when we are able to resolve the puzzles of life. One of the favourite activities of the Anglo-Saxons was setting riddles to while away the long northern nights. More recently, the huge popular fascination with works of detective fiction points to the continuing interest in unravelling mysteries. Writers such as Sir Arthur Conan Doyle, Agatha Christie, Erle Stanley Gardner and Dorothy L. Sayers built their reputations on being able to hold their readers' interest as countless mysterious murder cases were solved before their eyes.

The essence of a good mystery novel is a series of clues. The mystery to be solved is virtually invariably a murder. Perhaps a body has been discovered in the library of an English country house or in a London club. The mystery writers set us alongside their fictional detectives as they try to make sense of what happened by uncovering clues. So what are these clues? Basically, a clue is 'a fact or idea that serves as a guide, or suggests a line of enquiry, in a problem or investigation'. In other words, it is an observation that sets off a way of thinking about a problem.

In *The Adventure of the Stockbroker's Clerk* (1892–93), Sir Arthur Conan Doyle introduces us to the great fictional detective Sherlock Holmes' ability to build up an overall picture of events based on small clues. He begins by relating how Holmes deduced that his colleague Dr Watson had been ill. As usual, the narrator of the passage is Watson himself; the opening speaker is Holmes:

'I perceive that you have been unwell lately. Summer colds are always a little trying.'

'I was confined to the house by a severe chill for three days last week. I thought, however, that I had cast off every trace of it.'

'So you have. You look remarkably robust.'

'How, then, did you know of it?'

'My dear fellow, you know my methods.'

'You deduced it, then?'

Sherlock Holmes

'Certainly.'

'And from what?'

'From your slippers.'

I glanced down at the new patent-leathers which I was wearing. 'How on earth –' I began, but Holmes answered my question before it was asked.

'Your slippers are new,' he said. 'You could not have had them more than a few weeks. The soles which you are at this moment presenting to me are slightly scorched. For a moment I thought they might have got wet and been burned in the drying. But near the instep there is a small circular wafer of paper with the shopman's hieroglyphics upon it. Damp would of course have removed this. You had, then, been sitting with your feet outstretched to the fire, which a man would hardly do even in so wet a June as this if he were in his full health.' Like all Holmes' reasoning the thing seemed simplicity itself when it was once explained. He read the thought upon my features, and his smile had a tinge of bitterness.

'I am afraid that I rather give myself away when I explain.' said he. 'Results without causes are much more impressive.'

It is, of course, easy to overlook clues. Something may take place which appears to be insignificant at the time and yet assumes a much greater

significance later, as its full meaning gradually becomes apparent. Conan Doyle's story *Silver Blaze*, which tells of how Sherlock Holmes investigates an attack on a valuable racehorse, is a case in point. The watchdog did not bark during the night in which the racehorse was wounded. Yet the full significance of this fact only became evident at a later stage in Holmes' investigation. The fact was observed but its significance only became apparent later, when Holmes pointed out that it could only mean that the dog knew the intruder.

Important though they are, clues are not, however, decisive. Taken individually, a clue can do little more than suggest. It cannot prove. Yet clues

can accumulate, pointing in a certain and definite direction. At times, they even point in different directions. Many of the more celebrated mystery novels of Agatha Christie rely on building up a series of clues that point in a number of directions, leaving the reader wondering how the mystery may be solved. At other times, the clues allow multiple solutions to mysteries. We then have to deal with the question of which of a number of possible solutions is the most probable.

In her famous mystery novel *The Unpleasantness at the Bellona Club* (1928), set in London's high society during the 1920s, Dorothy L. Sayers opens the chapter describing Lord Peter Wimsey's breakthrough in the mystery surrounding the puzzling death of General Fentiman with the following words:

> 'What put you on to this poison business?' [Detective Inspector Parker] asked.
>
> 'Aristotle, chiefly,' replied Wimsey. 'He says, you know, that one should always prefer the probable impossible to the improbable possible. It was possible, of course, that the General should have died off in that neat way at the most confusing moment. But how much nicer and more probable that the whole thing had been stage-managed.'

Wimsey here had to make a judgment concerning which of a number of possible solutions to the mystery of General Fenniman's death was the most likely.

We face similar problems in trying to make sense of the universe and our place within it. We are surrounded by clues, some of which seem to point to one explanation and others in a very different direction. Some suggest that there is indeed a supreme being who created the universe and endowed it with purpose. Others seem to call this into question.

So what sort of clues are we talking about? One clue is provided by the natural sciences, especially physics and cosmology. Here, we find a remarkable degree of ordering within the universe, which can be expressed concisely and elegantly in mathematical forms. The fact that so much of the deep structure of the universe can be represented mathematically points to something remarkable about both the universe itself and to the ability of the human mind to understand it. It is almost as if the human mind has been designed to grasp the patterns and structures of the cosmos.

Albert Einstein (1879–1955) appreciated this point. In 1907, Einstein began to develop a new approach that he believed would explain a discrepancy which had been observed in the behaviour of the planet Mercury. This planet moved in a way which did not correspond with the predictions of classical astronomy, based on the ideas of Isaac Newton. In November 1915, Einstein finally discovered the theory of general relativity, which could be expressed beautifully in mathematical terms. But it was more than just a beautiful theory – it precisely accounted for the discrepancy in Mercury's movements. It was clear to Einstein that something deeply significant about the universe had been expressed in that theory. Was this not a clue to the universe reflecting the mind of God?

A second clue is provided by what is sometimes called the 'fine-tuning' of the universe. The structure of the universe is determined by a series of 'fundamental constants' that shape its contours and development. Had these been different, the universe would have taken a very different form – and life, as we know it, could not have emerged. The fabric of the universe seems to have been designed to establish the possibility of life. Perhaps this is entirely accidental. After all, our universe has to take some shape and form. Why not this one? Yet many pause for thought at this point. Could this really be accidental? Is it a pure coincidence that the laws of nature are such that life is possible? Might this not be an important clue to the nature and destiny of humanity?

Another clue is provided by the deep human longing for significance. It seems that nothing in this world really possesses the capacity to satisfy us. There is an emptiness within human nature, which cries out for fulfilment and meaning. Yet nothing created and transient seems able to meet this need. For Blaise Pascal, the only thing that could fill this abyss within human nature was a personal encounter with God. We find a similar theme in Augustine of Hippo (AD 354–430), who penned the following prayer to God: 'You have made us for yourself, and our heart is restless until it finds its rest in you.'

Another prayer to make the same point is due to Anselm of Canterbury (1033–1109), one of the greatest thinkers of the Middle Ages: 'Lord, give me what you have made me want; I praise and thank you for the

desire that you have inspired; perfect what you have begun, and grant me what you have made me long for'. For these writers, the deep human sense of longing has its origins in God, and can only find its fulfilment in God. God is the name of the one we have been looking for all our lives, without knowing it.

But other clues seem to point in another direction. For many, the presence of pain and suffering in the world seems to suggest that there cannot be a God. How, it may be asked, could a loving God allow such suffering to take place? This might not be a problem if God were not to be loving and to care for the creation. Yet Christianity insists that God is properly described as 'loving'. This important and profound belief would seem to be called into question by the pain of the world.

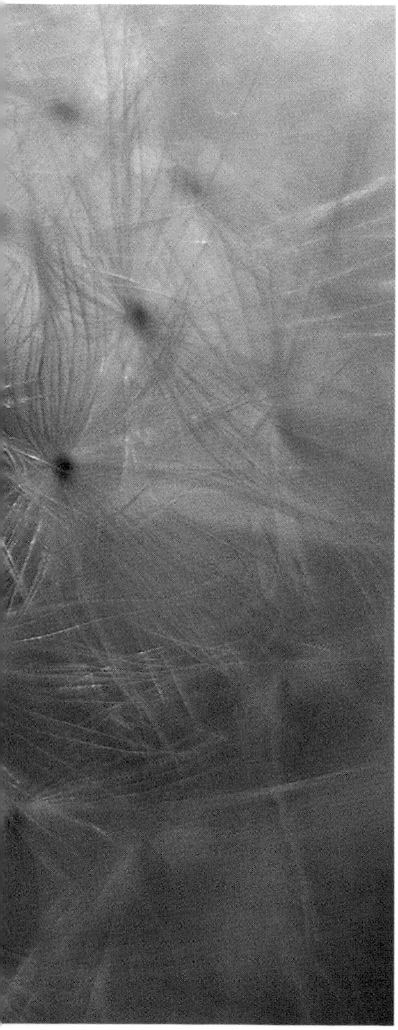

This process of gathering clues could be continued indefinitely. Yet the point that emerges is clear. Some aspects of the world seem to point to a divine creator; others seem to point away from him. The picture is not clear. The same problem, of course, emerges from the endless debate over whether the existence of God can be proved or disproved. Atheists and believers alike find it impossible to clinch their case through argument. At best, they can show that their position is plausible. But decisive proof of any kind is lacking.

Some refuse to recognize the

ambiguity of the situation. There has never been any shortage of people who will tell us that the evidence is totally persuasive, and that – unless we are complete fools – we will accept that there is no meaning in life, and no God behind this world. Some argue that atheism is the only logically and scientifically respectable worldview. Yet this overlooks the inconvenient fact that the truth claims of atheism simply cannot be proved. How do we know that there is no God? The simple fact of the matter is that atheism is a faith, which draws conclusions that go beyond the available evidence.

Boris Pasternak (1890–1960), the noted Russian writer and thinker who penned the novel *Dr Zhivago*, is an eloquent witness to this perhaps surprising point. Although initially highly enthusiastic about the Russian Revolution, he became disaffected with it because of the impact its harsh atheistic philosophy had upon people. He wrote these words in expressing his disillusionment: 'I am an atheist who has lost his faith'. Others will tell us with equal confidence that the evidence we see in nature is unequivocally in favour of the existence of some kind of God. It's all so simple. Only a fool would disagree.

It is hardly surprising that many are attracted to simple solutions to complex problems. Yet these rightly cause suspicion. We have become cynical of solutions that are too neat and claim to explain everything. We are as weary as we are wary of too-confident answers to difficult questions. The world we experience is just too messy and fuzzy to fit completely into the orderly systems that some crave and others fear. We have to learn to live in an untidy world in which we are not certain of everything – a world in which there are unanswered questions. Some panic at this thought. How can we live when we cannot be confident of anything? The only certainty of our age seems to be that there is no certainty at all. Yet even this confident assertion contradicts itself – like the statement that Bertrand Russell recalled seeing written on a college blackboard: 'All statements written on this blackboard are false.'

The reality of the situation is that there are few things that can be known with absolute certainty – and these generally take the form of tautologies. In other words, they are true by definition. For example, we can accept the truth of the following statement without any hesitation whatsoever:

The whole is greater than the part.

Once the meaning of the words 'whole' and 'part' has been grasped, the truth of the statement can be accepted immediately. Yet it can be argued without any difficulty that this statement is merely true by definition. It is true because of the relationship of the words 'whole' and 'part'. It adds nothing to our knowledge, merely restating what is already established.

A more subtle example is provided by the following statement, which may take a little longer to appreciate:

It is impossible for a man to marry his widow's sister.

At first sight, this might seem like an old-fashioned moralist taking a strong line on the ethics of marriage. On closer examination, however, it is nothing of the sort. The statement has nothing to do with ethics, or social acceptability. It has to do with the sheer practicality of death, which brings all human activity to an abrupt end. A man cannot marry his widow's sister precisely because a 'widow' is defined as 'a woman who has lost her husband by death'.

We have to learn to live with the fact that we cannot be certain of many of the most important things about life. We can be certain that 2 + 2 = 4; but that is hardly going to give us a reason to live and die, or cause our hearts to beat a little faster with excitement. Yet with the greater questions of life, we have to learn to live with a degree of uncertainty. Tennyson captures this dilemma perfectly in his poem 'The Ancient Sage' (1885):

For nothing worthy proving can be proven,
  nor yet disproven: wherefore thou be wise,
  cleave ever to the sunnier side of doubt.

For Tennyson, anything that was worth believing could not be proved with certainty. It involved a leap of faith – a recognition that the clues to the meaning of the universe do not provide an invincible case for a meaningless cosmos or one brought into being by a caring and loving God. Perhaps we can give up and walk away from the big questions that are raised. Yet in the end, this does not really satisfy us. Might not we be missing out on something important – and even exciting?

3 The Big Picture and the Best Explanation

We long to make sense of the world, putting together the clues we find around us to give a persuasive and attractive understanding of things. Yet we live in a world of competing explanations, a supermarket of ideas, all claiming to be what we are really seeking. One explanation is that we are here by accident. When we have completed our biologically determined role, we have no further purpose and die. Another and rather different explanation is that we have been created by a loving God, who has stooped down to meet us and bring us home to him.

So how can we even begin to make an informed choice here? Some worldviews are just too neat to be credible, making us suspicious precisely because they are so ambitious. Others seem more realistic, honestly acknowledging that there are some things that we may never fully understand, certain facts that do not seem to fit easily with their beliefs. The world just seems too fuzzy and messy to fit into neat categories. Worldviews sometimes blind us to realities, as Shakespeare seems to suggest in *Hamlet*:

> There are more things in heaven and earth, Horatio,
> than are dreamt of in your philosophy.

We long to see the 'big picture'. Yet we can at best only discern its individual parts. There are plenty of clues scattered throughout this world to allow us to conjecture about what that big picture looks like. But we never get to see it in its totality. There is always going to be an element of doubt, a degree of uncertainty, to what that big picture looks like. How can we, creatures who

are trapped in space and time, ever break through to catch a glimpse of the greater scheme of things of which we are a part? It is as if there was a great drama being played out on a stage, and we hear nothing more than echoes of its dialogue and dim reflections of the actors. We know that we are somehow involved in that drama, yet cannot fully understand what is going on. It is like someone who has camped at the base of a great range of mountains. What lies beyond them? At night, she sees light coming from the far side of the peaks and is able to hear the distant murmur of the music of the land beyond the mountains. There is something there, beyond those peaks. But what?

One of the great dreams of the Renaissance was to see that big picture. Might it be possible to draw aside the curtain that prevents us from seeing the drama? One of the most famous illustrations to emerge from the Renaissance shows an astronomer who has achieved his life's dream. He is able to gaze through the heavens and catch a glimpse of the celestial mechanics which keep the universe in place. Paul the apostle expressed a similar idea many centuries earlier. Now, he wrote, we only see things obscurely, as if they were dimly reflected to us through a mirror. But one day, he declares, we will see things as they really are (1 Corinthians 13:12). Things that don't seem to fit the theory might then slip into place.

So how can we begin to make sense of our world of apparent contradictions? Many would agree that the most successful human intellectual investigations of the world have been undertaken by the natural sciences. While the achievements of the natural sciences can easily be overstated by their well-meaning advocates, it is clear that they have important insights that can help us as we try to make sense of things. As the night sky has figured prominently in our reflections thus far, we may begin by considering the events which resulted from the discovery of the planet Uranus in 1781.

Until the 1780s, it was believed that there were only six planets in the solar system – Mercury, Venus, Earth, Mars, Jupiter and Saturn. The discovery of Uranus by Sir William Herschel was widely seen as a major intellectual achievement, a new discovery to be ranked alongside that of the finding of the Americas. The horizons of human knowledge had been raised yet again. However, as the orbit of the new planet was plotted over the next decades, it became clear that there were some problems. The planet did not seem to be behaving as predicted, on the basis of Isaac Newton's laws of planetary motion.

So what was wrong? One possibility was that the entire Newtonian theory of planetary motion was flawed and would have to be abandoned. This would have been a major problem. By the 1780s, Newton's account of the solar system was widely agreed to be the 'big picture'. This was seen as the most reliable account of the behaviour of the universe then available. It made sense of just about everything known about planetary movements up to that point. The movements of Uranus, however, did not seem to fit. Might the 'big picture' be wrong after all?

There was, however, another way of approaching the anomalous behaviour of Uranus. This was to argue that Newton's 'big picture' was basically correct. It did not need to be abandoned. The curious behaviour of Uranus could eventually be explained within the existing theory. Suppose there was yet another planet beyond Uranus, which was having a distorting impact upon its orbit?

The mathematicians got to work. They assumed that Newton's ideas did not need to be abandoned or revised. An additional hypothesis was needed – namely, that there was a hitherto unknown planet beyond Uranus. In the end, the mathematicians predicted where in the night skies this new planet must lie. On 23 September 1846, the new planet was observed close to where it had been predicted. It was named Neptune.

The story is well known but its implications need

careful study. The unusual behaviour of the planet Uranus was a clue. But a clue to what? It could be interpreted in a number of ways. Taken by itself, it proved nothing. Perhaps it might have pointed to the need to abandon Newton's ideas about planetary motion. Or perhaps it indicated something new – that led to an expansion of our knowledge while keeping Newton's basic ideas intact. But which?

We find this same issue emerging time and time again as we try to make sense of the world. The deep sense of longing and dissatisfaction which so many experience is unquestionably a clue to the meaning of our universe and especially our place within it. But what does this clue point to? Does it point to the ability of human nature to shield itself from the grim

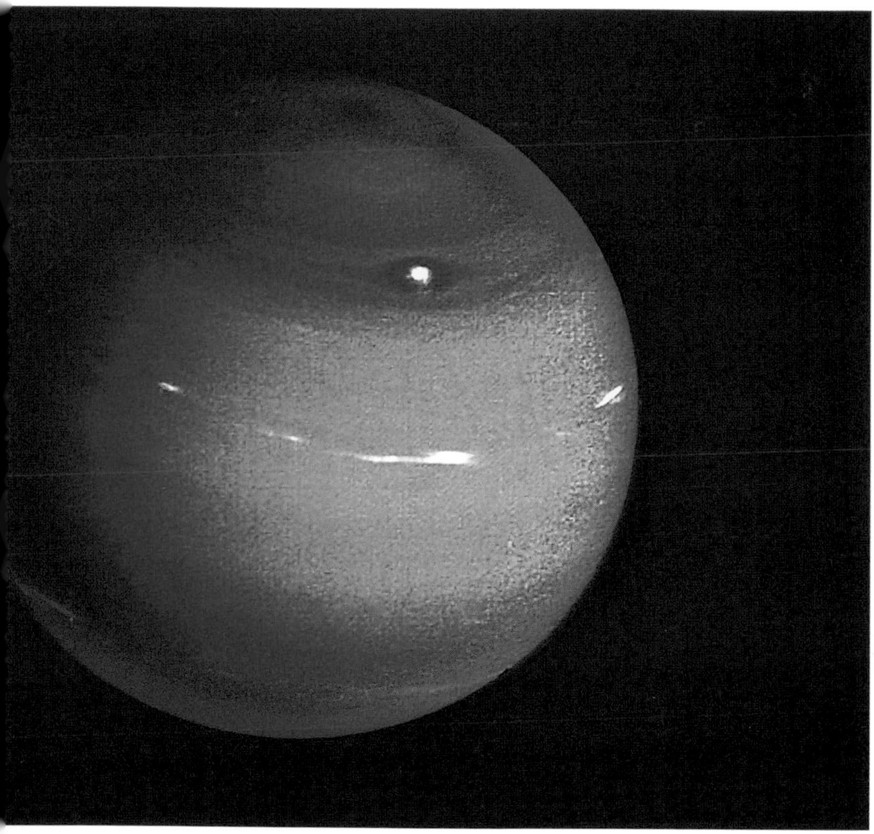

NEPTUNE

reality of a hopeless and dying universe? Or is it a prompting to discover the reality of a God who alone is able to meet our deepest needs and longings? Is this spiritual longing that hovers around the edges of our experience some recollection of a long-lost home that we are meant to rediscover and enter?

A similar question arises if we try another approach to making sense of our situation. For many, Jesus Christ holds the key to the meaning of life. Making sense of Christ might well be a means to seeing something of the 'big picture' that is so tantalizingly hard to grasp. As we read the Gospel narratives of the life of Christ, we are confronted with countless clues to his identity and his significance for us. Taken individually, these can seem ambiguous. Taken together, however, they build up to give something rather more exciting.

The Gospel of Mark's account of how Jesus healed a paralytic (Mark 2:1–12) illustrates this point well. In healing the paralytic, Jesus tells him that his 'sins are forgiven'. This provokes outrage and astonishment on the part of some experts in the Jewish law, who were onlookers to this scene. For these experts, Jesus' words were certainly a major clue to his identity and significance. 'He is blaspheming! Who can forgive sins but God alone!' (Mark 2:7). Their conclusion was that Jesus had made a deeply offensive and outrageous claim concerning himself. What human being had the right to claim to act as God? The clue pointed to Jesus being deluded or dangerous.

Yet there is another way of making sense of that clue. Christ had no right or authority whatsoever to speak those words if he was simply a human being. But what if Christ were more than this? What if he were – as Christians have always insisted is the case – God incarnate, the living God entering into human history, in order to share our pain and sorrow? Would not he have been entirely justified in claiming to forgive sins – in doing something that only God can do?

The clue provided by Jesus' words here was thus open to a number of interpretations. It might suggest that he was unstable, deluded, muddled or confused. Or it might point to something profound and deeply significant about Jesus, with profound implications for the way we think about God, and the way in which that God relates to us. But which?

The great question that emerges from our reflections is often referred to as 'inference to the best explanation'. It is a classic debate in the philosophy of science, and has immense importance for any attempt to make sense of the world. Philosophers of science stress that the interpretation of the world is far from clear-cut. There are many ways of making sense of what we observe, many theories which seek to explain the puzzles and enigmas of human experience. Yet deciding which is right is far from simple. Time after time, judgment has to be suspended. In case after case, there turns out to be no knock-down argument, no 'decisive experiment', that can resolve the issue once and for all.

The popular understanding of how the natural sciences work bears little relation to this. Many have the idea that it takes one apparent piece of contradictory evidence to refute a theory. The reality is very different. Natural scientists are happy to live with anomalies and enigmas that cannot presently be explained by their theories, but which they believe will one day be resolved by further advances in our understanding.

A classic example of this trend can be seen in William Prout's hypothesis of 1815, which argued that all the chemical elements of the universe – carbon, nitrogen, oxygen, sodium and so on – were basically made up of hydrogen. On the basis of this hypothesis, it would be expected that the atomic weights of the elements would be integral multiples of that of hydrogen. This was certainly plausible. For example, the atomic weight of oxygen was almost exactly 16 times that of hydrogen. However, the very precise measurements of atomic weights by the Swedish chemist Jöns Berzelius later that century called Prout's ideas into question. Berzelius showed that a number of elements clearly possessed non-integral atomic weights – such as chlorine, with a weight of 35.45. This was widely seen as a decisive contradiction of Prout's hypothesis. It was abandoned by most scientists as inconsistent with observational data.

However, the discovery of isotopes in 1910 reversed this judgment completely. It was established that a number of elements existed with different atomic weights, while having the same atomic numbers. Chlorine, for example, had isotopes with atomic weights of 35, 36 and 37. Each of these isotopes possessed an atomic weight which was an integral multiple of that of hydrogen. Suddenly, Prout's hypothesis was credible again. The data that had once seemed to be a decisive refutation of the theory now ended up supporting the idea.

Charles Darwin

The details of this piece of natural science need not trouble us further at this point. The real issue concerns the way in which loose ends, inconsistences and anomalies can be dealt with by worldviews. People are prepared to hold on to a theory that manages to make sense of lots of things, even though there may seem to be some serious difficulties with it. In the end, it is argued, these difficulties will be resolved – as with Prout's theory – even though it may not be clear yet how this will take place.

This point has long been accepted by natural scientists. The theory of natural selection put forward by Charles Darwin (1809–82) was prompted by a number of clues, including the distinctive characteristics of the finches he observed on the Galápagos Islands during the famous voyage of HMS *Beagle*. On the basis of these clues, he put forward a theory that he believed accounted for many of them. Many, certainly – but by no means all. Darwin was aware that his theory could not account for many observations and that it seemed to be contradicted by others. Yet he did not believe that this caused him to abandon his theories. As he wrote in concluding his work *The Origin of Species* (1859):

> A crowd of difficulties will have occurred to the reader. Some of them are so grave that to this day I can never reflect on them without being staggered; but, to the best of my judgment, the greater number are only apparent, and those that are real are not, I think, fatal to my theory.

Darwin was perfectly prepared to live with this unresolved tension. He believed that there was enough evidence available to suggest that his was the best explanation of what he observed. Given this faith in his theory, he felt he could cope with the obvious difficulties of contradictions, anomalies and loose ends.

Anyone who adopts a worldview finds that they are confronted with exactly the same issues. There are difficulties and anomalies alongside the many clues and pointers that are supportive of their position. It is a matter of having faith. It is about trusting that the many merits of the worldview compensate for those areas in which it seems to be weaker.

So how might one go about evaluating a worldview? Clearly, one issue must be its ability to make sense of things. We must have reason to believe that it is right. What reasons may be offered for believing that it is telling the truth? That it is reliable? In the next chapter, we shall begin to explore this issue in a little more detail.

The Quest for Wisdom

Plato once defined a philosopher as someone who took pleasure in the truth. Yet these are not especially easy times for those questing after this truth. The greatest question of life sometimes seems to be not what we know but how we know anything at all. Why are we here? Where are we going? What is the point of it all? Many have dreamed of systems of knowledge based on unshakeable certainties. In centuries past, people looked to human reason to provide certain answers to the great mysteries of human life. Yet as time passed, that dream began to fade. The Enlightenment – that great 'Age of Reason' – led directly to some of the darker moments of our history. Marxism and Nazism, two of the most reviled worldviews of the 20th century, are both stepchildren of the Age of Reason. Their parents might like to disown them; the family resemblance, however, is unmistakable.

Faced with the past tyranny of reason, many have responded by suggesting that the idea of 'truth' is a dangerous illusion. There is no such thing, we are told, as truth – only the ideas and values to which we take a liking and choose to build into our views of the world. We make the decisions. We grant ideas the privilege of impacting on our lives. We pick and mix. All ideas are equally valid, so we are free to create a fusion of ideas of our choice. Something is true if we like it – if it works for us. Like a magpie lining its nest with shiny objects it found attractive, we construct our own mental worlds, furnishing them with ideas that appeal to us. Beliefs become like wallpaper; we choose them and apply them according to our taste.

So why has this idea that all beliefs are equally valid arisen, and gained such credibility in Western culture? The main reason for this seems to be a fierce reaction against worldviews such as Nazism and Marxism, which insisted that there was only one way of viewing the world – namely, theirs. Anyone who failed to conform to their views was a deviationist, a reactionary, or was mentally ill. The best way of dealing with such awkward people was by eliminating them, imprisoning them, or forcibly confining them to mental hospitals. As the full horror of Stalin's liquidation of political dissenters in the 1930s, and Hitler's extermination camps of the 1940s, became clear, many took the view that the best way of preventing totalitarianism was to insist that all views were equally valid. The best way of preventing political totalitarianism was by discouraging anything that led one group of people to see themselves as superior to others.

The first casualty of this well-intentioned strategy was truth. To claim to tell the truth, it was argued, was to claim authority over people. It was the first step towards oppressing others. Anyone who disagreed with you was either stupid or mad – and hence marked out as inferior. The only way to avoid this was to insist that all views – political, religious and intellectual – were to be treated with equal favour.

The intention of this approach was praiseworthy. If all views are equally valid, we ought to be able to avoid the pitfalls of Stalin and the Nazis. Yet there is a price-tag attached to this strategy. Are all viewpoints really equally valid? Surely one of the skills that human beings are meant to develop is the ability to distinguish between truth and falsehood – even when that falsehood is sincerely believed? Surely a quest for truth lies at the heart of the human desire to make sense of things? Matthew Arnold (1822–88) summed up the values of a lost generation in his *Stanzas from the Grande Chartreuse* (1855):

> For rigorous teachers seized my youth,
> and purged its faith, and trimm'd its fire,
> show'd me the high, white star of Truth,
> there bade me gaze, and there aspire.

Yet many today would regard a concern with truth as misguided. Who cares?

This, at any rate, is the public face of Western culture, which is repeated like a sociological mantra by the prophets and gurus of our age. Yet deep down, nobody really believes that all ideas are equally valid. They may pay lip-service to this ideal, aware that its widespread acceptance in the corridors of power – academic, social and political – will do some good for their careers. But the weakness of the approach is painfully obvious. Take the following opinion: 'The Nazi holocaust never really happened'. There are few who would allow that this view is as valid as the belief that there was indeed a holocaust and that we ought to make sure that there is not another. After all, it was precisely this concern to avoid a future holocaust that led to the insistence that 'all views are equally valid' in the first place.

Yet the superficial insistence that all viewpoints are equally valid legitimates this and other seriously defective readings of history. How can we learn from history, if we can simply rewrite that history to suit our agendas and interests? If 'history' is just something that we construct, we are at liberty to construct the version that we feel most comfortable with. In the past, history was something written by the winning side; nowadays, history can be seen from any angle that happens to suit people's personal preferences.

It is important to honour the concern that lies behind this dismissive

attitude to truth. Nobody wants to encourage the rise of totalitarianism. Yet paradoxically this dismissal of the notion of truth can easily encourage the rise of exactly this phenomenon. Denying that Stalin liquidated millions of Russians during the 1930s, or that Hitler sent millions to the gas chambers in the 1940s, is opening the door to the re-emergence of such regimes. It may seem to some to be a playful and harmless academic game. The reality is much more sinister. Being careless with the truth opens the way to enslavement by falsehoods.

The great task of classical philosophy was to somehow conform the human mind to reality. It did this by stressing the ideas of accountability, knowledge and virtue. The challenge is to force the human mind to come to terms with the real world around it, and somehow make sense of it. The interpretations the mind offered were to be judged against the reality they tried to grasp and represent.

Yet some today would dispute this, arguing that we are free to make any choices we like. 'There are no facts, only interpretations' (Friedrich Nietzsche). The idea that there is some 'absolute' that we are under an obligation to discover and express is ridiculed. Yet, as Hitler's extermination

JOSEPH STALIN AT THE MAY DAY PARADE IN MOSCOW'S RED SQUARE, 8 MAY 1952

camps and Stalin's liquidation programmes make dreadfully clear, to relativize the absolute is merely to 'absolutize' the relative. Totalitarianism can only arise with the overthrow of its final and greatest opponent – a God who negates the absolute autonomy of humanity and who holds it accountable for its actions.

Natural scientists have never taken this kind of relativist outlook with any great seriousness, to the immense irritation of its proponents. For natural scientists, the important thing is to investigate the world as accurately as possible and confirm our beliefs by rigorous testing. For example, the chemical composition of water is H_2O. How do we know this? By a series of experiments which have repeatedly demonstrated that a molecule of water consists of two hydrogen atoms and one oxygen atom. It does not matter whether these experiments are carried out by women or by men, or by Anglo-Saxons or by Asians. The chemical composition of water is independent of the gender, race and social status of the investigator.

This poses something of a problem to those who insist that all views are equally valid. The critic of the traditional view might argue that it rests upon an obsession with oppression and domination. It is, our imaginary critic might declare, outrageous that hydrogen should be dominated by oxygen in this way. In a more caring and equitable world, hydrogen and oxygen would exist together in harmony and equality. Therefore we need to reject the traditional formula for water as H_2O as resting on outdated feudal assumptions and embrace the liberating idea of the absolute parity of hydrogen and oxygen in water. The chemical formula of water therefore ought not to be H_2O but should instead be the more egalitarian H_2O_2 – that is, that there are two hydrogen atoms and two oxygen atoms in a molecule of water.

Now let us hope that this is such a bizarre and brainless idea that nobody would be tempted to agree with it. The proposal founders utterly on the rock of empirical investigation. Although the idea might appeal to those who believed that the world ought to be constructed according to their personal beliefs and values, the reality is that the world feels no particular reason to conform to those. It possesses its own structures and rationality that we need to discover – rather than imposing our own preconceptions of what ought to be right upon it. The natural sciences aim to uncover the world as it is rather than impose our own prejudices upon it.

People do not believe that the chemical composition of water is H_2O because of some obsession with dominance, infatuation with the number '2', or misguided trust in the authority of white-coated laboratory workers. They believe it because it rests upon rigorous experimental evidence that may be repeated under carefully monitored conditions, which demonstrates that this formula – and no other formula – corresponds to water as it actually is. As it happens, there is indeed a chemical which corresponds to the formula H_2O_2. It is not, however, water. Hydrogen peroxide – as the chemical corresponding to the formula H_2O_2 is known – is a powerful oxidizing agent, suitable for bleaching human hair and powering liquid rocket motors. It is most emphatically not suitable for drinking, or sustaining human life!

Perhaps the most puzzling wisdom of our age is that something can be 'true for me' but not 'true for you', often repeated as if it were a mantra guaranteeing personal tranquillity and fulfilment for its believers. But is it true? Is there the slightest reason for suggesting that my firm belief that the chemical formula of water is H_2O is not valid for anyone else? Another person might legitimately inform me that this might well be my perception, but that their viewpoint that water has the formula H_2O_2 is just as good. Another might reply that, since water is really the psychic teardrops of tantric beings, it does not have a chemical formula. And as that is true for them, nobody has any right to disturb their beliefs on this matter.

But we could take this further by thinking about some less amusing possibilities. Consider the person who argues that it was entirely proper to put millions of Jews to death in gas chambers during the Nazi period – and that it is still right to do so. Such a belief, if sincerely held, may certainly be 'true for them'. But can it be allowed to pass unchallenged for that reason? Are they as valid as beliefs such as that one ought to live in peace and tolerance with one's neighbours, rather than throwing them into death camps?

Or consider the person who believes, passionately and sincerely, that it is an excellent thing to burn a widow alive on her late husband's funeral pyre. This belief was widespread and popular (especially, I understand, among males) in parts of India during the 19th century. It was widely and presumably sincerely held. So can it be left unchallenged? The wisdom of our age seems to be that you can think what you like. This may well be fine when dealing with personal private beliefs. But what if these private beliefs become public policy?

However unfashionable it may be to say so, the truth of a worldview is important. It may be consoling to believe that we can avoid all the dangers of the world by placing crystal pyramids at strategic points throughout our homes. Yet no matter how consoling such a belief may be, there will come a day when its obvious weaknesses will be put to the test. We can cocoon ourselves in all kinds of beliefs of personal immortality and invulnerability. Yet if they rest on flimsy foundations, they cannot be sustained.

To have no hope in life is a terrible thing; to build that life on a false hope is still worse. A day of reckoning will dawn when those soothing illusions will be stripped away. Surely we need to build our lives upon beliefs that may be relied upon, rather than something superficially attractive, yet fundamentally flawed? It is no accident that many young people adopt worldviews that they abandon as they grow older, realizing that the realities of life simply do not support these ambitious philosophies. We have every right to interrogate worldviews, asking them and their adherents what reasons may be given for trusting them. Why should we rely upon them? How can we know that we are not being deluded or deceived?

History offers us some sad reminders of the importance of this point. In 1525 Thomas Müntzer led a revolt of German peasants against their political masters. On the morning of the decisive encounter between the peasant mob and the armies of the German princes, Müntzer promised that those who followed him would be unscathed by the weapons of their enemies. They were guaranteed personal invulnerability on account of their trust in him. Encouraged by this attractive and meaningful belief, the peasants entered into battle with the forces of the German establishment.

The outcome was nothing less than a catastrophe for those unfortunate peasants. Six thousand of them were slaughtered in the ensuing battle. Barely a handful escaped. Their belief in invulnerability was shown to be a crude and cruel lie, without any foundation in truth. The last hours of that pathetic group of trusting men rested on an utter illusion. It was only when the first salvoes cut some of their number to ribbons that they realized that they had been deceived. These poor people had unquestionably been offered hope. Yet, as events turned out, it was a false hope.

It may be tempting to base our lives upon something that initially seems attractive. Some live their lives like intellectual butterflies, flitting from one

flower to the next, never remaining in one place. Yet for most, the issue is to search out the best possible worldview and to allow that to give meaning and security to our lives. The biblical image of the rock is especially important, as it points to something that is stable, capable of withstanding the storms and waves that will crash against us throughout our lives. We want and we need something that will give resilience to life. It must be true, worthy of our trust.

However, as we shall see, there are many things in life that are unquestionably correct, yet have little or no conceivable relevance to our lives. We long for security, stability and meaning. How often has life been compared with a house, which must be built upon secure foundations if it is to survive? We have already noted the Gospel parable of the 'house built upon the rock' and the need to ensure that our lives are based upon something that we believe to be reliable and trustworthy. But is that enough?

Consider each of the following statements, each of which is correct at the time of writing this book (2000):

✤ The 1980 population of Mercer County, Illinois, USA, was 19,286.

✤ The rainfall for the month September 1999 for the southern English coastal resort of Exmouth was 117 millimetres.

✤ The *Connecticut Courant*, the oldest American newspaper in continuous existence to the present, was launched at Hartford by Thomas Green in 1764.

✤ The capital city of the Republic of Mali is Bamako.

✤ I currently have 18 books open on my desk in front of me.

Each of these statements is correct. Perhaps they might be exciting to someone who believes that you can achieve fulfilment in life by simply accumulating facts. Personally, I'm not so sure.

Just how important are these facts? I do indeed have 18 books open on my desk today; tomorrow, I will probably replace some on my shelves, or perhaps open some more. But it is not really the kind of thing that is going to turn someone's life inside out. It might indeed be useful for someone stranded in West Africa to know that the capital city of Mali is Bamako. Yet the political instability of the region is such that this nugget of information may become out of date alarmingly quickly. And yes, there are people who get very seriously excited about population and rainfall figures, just as there are some people who derive deep satisfaction from collecting the postage stamps issued by the British Empire during the reign of Queen Victoria. But there must be a serious question concerning how important these matters really are. Truth does not guarantee relevance.

The writers of the ancient world knew this, and made a distinction which our modern era seems to have forgotten – the distinction between 'knowledge' and 'wisdom'. Knowledge is the accumulation of facts; wisdom is being transformed on the basis of what is true, and really matters. In the language of the classical tradition, wisdom is affective – that is, it changes the one who seeks it by bringing that person into its orbit and under its transformative influence. Wisdom changes people. 'Knowledge comes, but wisdom lingers' (Tennyson).

We need something that we can trust, that can be relied upon – something that is going to make a difference to our lives, rather than just weary us with yet more facts to add to our overburdened memories and lives. This idea developed in both the Old and New Testaments. The basic meaning of the Hebrew word normally translated as 'truth' or 'true' (as in 'the true God') is 'something which can be relied upon', or 'someone who can be trusted'. Truth thus is not simply about being right; it is about trustworthiness. It is a relational concept, pointing us to someone who is totally worthy of our trust. We are not being asked to know yet another fact but to enter into a relationship with one who is able to sustain and comfort us.

This idea is developed in what is for many people one of the most memorable of the Gospel parables. The parable of the 'house built on the rock' tells of two individuals, one who chose to build a house upon sand and the other upon rock (Matthew 7:24–27). When the storms came, the house built upon the sand collapsed, being incapable of withstanding the forces that buffeted it. The house built upon the rock survived. The point being made has become something of a platitude for many. However, as a former British Prime Minister, Stanley Baldwin, once commented, 'a platitude is simply a truth repeated until people get tired of hearing it'. We need to base our lives on something secure and reliable. When someone finds the right thing to trust, they can let the rest of their life look after itself.

In what follows, we will explore one way of looking at things that seems to have considerable promise in this respect.

5 THE GREAT NARRATIVE OF OUR DESTINY

We are haunted by the need to make sense of things. There are many great accounts of our origin and destiny and countless explanations of how the world is as we find it. Some argue that it is impossible to make an informed choice and commend permanent neutrality on all such issues. Yet a cynic might argue that this is little more than a refusal to engage with the great issues of life, draped for the sake of intellectual decency with some rather skimpy shreds of a relativist philosophy.

In the end, we have to give some thought to such things, even if in a cautious and hesitant manner. It is easy to see why some are reluctant to commit themselves in advance of such reflection. So let us conduct a mental exercise, a thought experiment. Let us play around with one of the great narratives of human destiny and see where it takes us. We will try it on and see how it fits. How well does it make sense of things? And what difference does it make? Suppose, just for the same of argument, that we suspend disbelief and try to get inside a major belief system. What does it teach and how do these ideas help us make sense of things?

Christianity holds that a loving God created this universe purposefully. We are not the result of some cosmic accident, but the intentional outcome of God's decision to create us. Now this is quite a dramatic statement to make and it is rich with implications. Before we try to explore its consequences, we need to spend a little more time wrestling with what that word 'create' means.

The Old Testament uses a number of helpful illustrations to help us make sense of this idea of creation. Creation can be compared with a master craftsman who designs and constructs a building. The wisdom of the creator can thus be seen in the ordering of the world, in much the same way as the wisdom of an architect can be seen in the design of a great building. Creation is thus about ordering, imposing structure upon reality.

This biblical understanding of creation resonates strongly with the discoveries of the natural sciences. The natural sciences are founded on the perception of explicable regularity to the world. In other words, the human mind is able to discern a pattern within nature, which is capable of being represented mathematically. There is something about the world, and the nature of the human mind as it reflects upon that world, that allows us to discern patterns within nature, for which explanations may be advanced and evaluated.

One of the most significant parallels between the natural sciences and Christianity is this fundamental conviction that the world is characterized by regularity and intelligibility. This perception of ordering and intelligibility is of immense significance, both at the scientific and religious levels. As the eminent physicist Paul Davies points out, 'in Renaissance Europe, the justification for what we today call the scientific approach to inquiry was the belief in a rational God whose created order could be discerned from a careful study of nature'.

CHRISTOPHER WREN

Nature thus bears witness to God's wisdom, just as a great building bears witness to the genius of its designer. St Paul's Cathedral, London, is one of the greatest works of the architect Sir Christopher Wren (1631–1723). The cathedral had to be rebuilt after the Great Fire of London (1666), and the task of designing the new building was entrusted to Wren. The great new building was finally completed in 1710 and remains one of the most famous landmarks of London. There is no memorial to Wren in that cathedral. In its place, there is an inscription over its north door: 'If you are looking for a memorial, look around you'. The genius and wisdom of the architect can be seen in what he built. In the same way, the wisdom of God can be discerned within the creation, which is a witness to the power and wisdom of its creator. 'The heavens are telling the glory of God!' (Psalm 19:1).

A second way of thinking about creation is to compare this with the creative actions of an artist – like someone painting a picture or composing a symphony. We might speak of such an artist 'putting a lot of herself into' the picture or music, meaning that the artistic creation in some way mirrors the nature and genius of the artist. Yet the same God who created the universe also created us. There is thus a created resonance between ourselves and the universe. We are enabled to hear the music of its creator and discern the hand of the creator within its beauty. It is part of the purpose of the creator that we should hear the music of the cosmos, and, through loving its harmonies, come to love their composer.

It is at this point that we need to pause and introduce one of the most challenging insights of a Christian understanding of creation. We are created 'in the image of God' (Genesis 1:26–27). Now the word 'image' suggests a similarity, a correspondence – but not an identity. There is some affinity between God and ourselves, resting on the fact that we have been created purposefully. We have been made to know God – that is to say, to know about God, and to enter into a relationship with God, as we might know a close and dear friend.

This insight is charged with explanatory potential. Why is it that the human mind is able to discern the pattern of the world? Why is it that there appears to be some correspondence between the rationality of the cosmos and our own rationality? If there were not, the universe would remain a mystery to us. Why is it that we are able to represent the structuring and ordering of the world in the language of mathematics when this is supposedly the free creation of the human mind?

The answers to all these questions converge – because we have been created with the ability to peer into the mind of God. If our reasoning has its source in God, it has the potential to lead us to its fountain-head. Even though it may be attenuated through our weakness and frailty, our created reason retains its God-given ability to guide us to its creator. The stream can point us to its source. And just as that flow of water cannot detach itself from its fountain-head, so the human mind has a created capacity to guide us home to God. The resonance between reason, the world and God is no accident; it is an integral aspect of the Christian doctrine of creation.

The human mind, some argue, is superbly capable of defending itself against thoughts that it finds troubling. There is always one more portcullis to lower, another drawbridge to raise, to prevent the intrusion of threatening ideas – such as personal extinction and the meaninglessness of the cosmic void. Yet equally it can be argued that the mind is finely tuned to discerning signals of transcendence, patterns within the world that point to our origins and destiny lying in God. On this view, God has created us to relate to him and, if we do not do so, we lose sight of our true goal and joy. We are designed to need God, as a computer is designed to run on electricity. God himself would thus be the ultimate food and fuel of authentic human existence. God does not offer us salvation and joy as if these could somehow be detached from his loving and caring presence. Without God, we are unfulfilled, precisely because we have been created with a God-shaped gap within us, which cries out to be filled with the luxurious presence of our creator. God has thus fashioned us in such a way that we may begin to gain at least a glimpse of his nature and being from the world around us.

This point was made at some length by Bonaventura (1221–74), a medieval philosopher and theologian with a keen eye for the importance of the creation as a guide to its creator:

> All the creatures of this sensible world lead the soul of the wise and contemplative person to the eternal God, since they are the shadows, echoes and pictures, the vestiges, images and manifestations of that

> most powerful, most wise and best first principle, of that eternal origin, light and fullness, of that productive, exemplary and order-giving Art. They are set before us for the sake of our knowing God, and are divinely given signs. For every creature is by its very nature a kind of portrayal and likeness of that eternal Wisdom.

If the world is indeed created, it follows that the beauty, goodness and wisdom of its creator are reflected, however dimly, in the world around us. All of us have known a sense of delight at the beauty of the natural world. Yet this is but a shadow of the beauty of its creator. We see what is good and realize that something still better lies beyond it. And what lies beyond is not an abstract, impersonal and unknowable force but a personal God who has created us in order to love and cherish us.

We have been made to relate to God – to know him. That is one of the most fundamental themes of the Christian faith. Without God, human existence will seem unfulfilled and empty. The creation has the potential to point to its creator. Yet it lacks the ability to satisfy our deepest longings. We have been made to long for God and only the living God can fulfil the longings that he has created.

Many have found that the awesome sight of the star-studded heavens evoke a sense of wonder, an awareness of transcendence, that is charged with spiritual significance. Yet the distant shimmering of stars does not itself create this sense of longing; it merely exposes what is already there. They are catalysts for our spiritual insights, revealing our emptiness and compelling us to ask whether and how this void might be filled. Might our true origins and destiny somehow lie beyond those stars? Might there not be a homeland, from which we are presently exiled and to which we secretly long to return? Might not our accumulation of discontentment and disillusionment with our present existence be a pointer to another land where our true destiny lies and which is able to make its presence felt now in this haunting way? Suppose that this is not where we are meant to be but that a better land is at hand? We don't belong here. We have somehow lost our way. Would not this make

our present existence both strange and splendid? Strange, because it is not where our true destiny lies; splendid, because it points ahead to where that real hope might be found.

The beauty of the night skies or a glorious sunset are important pointers to the origins and the ultimate fulfilment of our heart's deepest desires. But if we mistake the signpost for what is signposted, we will attach our hopes and longings to lesser goals, which cannot finally quench our thirst for meaning. This enigmatic thought was expressed lyrically by the Russian writer and Orthodox priest Gregory Petrov in his 'Hymn of Thanksgiving', written shortly before he died in a Soviet labour camp in 1940:

O Lord, how lovely it is to be your guest.
Breezes full of scents; mountains reaching to the skies;
waters like boundless mirrors, reflecting the sun's golden rays and the scudding clouds.
All nature murmurs mysteriously, breathing the depth of tenderness.
Birds and beasts of the forest bear the imprint of your love.
Blessed is mother earth, in your passing loveliness, which awakens our yearning for the happiness that will last for ever,
in the eternal native land where, amid beauty that will never grow old, the cry rings out: Alleluia!

Petrov clearly found immense consolation in these thoughts. The natural world that surrounded the inhuman and degrading life of the labour camp pointed to a future homeland free of oppression and pain. The forests, mountains and lakes around the camp signalled a future hope that illuminated and transfigured his present situation.

It is, of course, easy to critique Petrov. Karl Marx – whose political philosophy, it may be added, led to Petrov being thrown into a labour camp in the first place – would have dismissed such thoughts as deluded dreams. They represent the 'opium of the people', the spurious creation of a human mind desperate to dull itself to the pain and tragedy of this harsh world. We will not comment further on the fact that Marx may legitimately be said to be held responsible for the grim predicament in which Petrov found himself, along with countless other miserable souls. There is a more important point to be made.

Marx argued that such consoling thoughts of a secure future homeland of the soul were totally illusory. They were an invention, designed to distract the human mind from a cruel reality. Yet our reflections in this chapter offer another way of looking at Petrov's future hope. If the human mind is indeed *capax Dei* – to use a classic phrase which means something like 'possessing an intrinsic ability to grasp something of God' – then Petrov's thoughts are entirely proper. They represent the natural and appropriate outcome of a distinct understanding of human nature and destiny. The God who created us to relate to, and to be with, him also created the universe around us, which points, hesitatingly yet meaningfully, to that same God.

Though the captive of a harsh political regime, Petrov found consolation in the signs of a future homeland around him, which reminded and reassured him of a future glory that would finally erase and banish his memories and experience of hell on earth. What consoled Petrov may merely intrigue others. Yet his line of thought must be taken seriously. Does what we now experience point to something that lies beyond it? Does our encounter with the world presage an encounter with another reality that is yet to come in all its fullness? Might stars, forests, mountains and lakes be a silent witness to a greater glory – a glory whose radiance will exceed anything we have hitherto known but which is dimly mirrored in its images and semblances? These haunting questions will not go away and will never be conclusively answered. Perhaps they are just gentle dreams and pleasant delusions, enabling us to cope with what might otherwise be unbearable. Then again, they might be clues to the mystery of life.

Yet we must pause at this point, and raise the issue we considered in the previous chapter. What difference do such thoughts make? Do they have the potential to affect us, to transform us? Or are they just interesting yet ultimately sterile ideas, which we might as well add to our accumulated thoughts as a stamp collector might mount a new item in his already burgeoning collection? What, in short, is the cash value of believing in this notion of creation?

Perhaps I can best explore this point by telling of my own experiences. As a young boy, I found myself fascinated with the night sky. I learned the names of the constellations, and tracked the slow movements of the planets against the background of the fixed stars. I even managed to construct a small telescope, which allowed me to observe the lunar craters, the moons of Jupiter and the rings of Saturn. It was all fascinating and at times I struggled to take in the wonders that I was observing. Yet at the same time, I found my stargazing made me despondent, rather than excited.

The more I learned about astronomy, the more I began to appreciate the vastness of the universe and the immensity of the distances between the stars. I found reflecting on those distances to be a melancholy affair. So distant were some of the bright stars of the night sky that their light took at least 100 years to reach Earth. And I would not be alive to witness this arrival. The span of human life seemed insignificantly brief, in comparison with the vast distances and timescales of the cosmos. I began to realize that the stars had become symbols of human transience for me. They offered intimations of mortality without bringing me hope.

My growing knowledge of astronomy helped me appreciate the beauty of the universe. Yet it was a melancholy beauty, in that I was unable to detach the glory of the heavens from the transience and fragility of the one observing that glory. It was as if the stars proclaimed the insignificance and transience of those they allowed to observe them.

Yet when I began to think of the world as created, my outlook changed entirely. Different perspectives were opened up for me. The stars, of course, remained as they were. Yet the way I viewed them altered radically. No longer

were they harbingers of transience. They were now symbols of a wisdom and care of a God who knew and loved me. The words of Psalm 8 seemed to sum things up so well:

> When I look at your heavens, the work of your fingers,
> the moon and the stars that you have established;
> what are human beings that you are mindful of them,
> mortals that you care for them?
> Yet you have made them a little lower than God,
> and crowned them with glory and honour.

The stars are signs of the providence of God, who knows them and calls them by name (Psalm 147:4) – just as he know us and calls us by name. No longer were the stars silent memorials of transience; they were brilliant heralds of the love of God. I was not alone in the universe but walked and lived in the presence of a God who knew me and would never forget me.

But how do we find this God? How can we draw close to him? Must we speak of the human quest for God – or might we be dealing with a God who comes in search of us? The ancient world gave extended thought to such questions and had some important answers to offer. So how does the kind of approach that we have been exploring relate to the wisdom of the past? We shall explore this in what follows.

6 Beyond the Wisdom of the Ancients

The ancient world witnessed the rise and fall of some of the noblest civilizations that the world has ever known. The great pyramids of Egypt, the hanging gardens of Babylon, the Parthenon of Athens and the Colossus of the island of Rhodes were singled out by writers of this era as representing some of the greatest achievements of the human spirit. Yet these great civilizations of the ancient world did more than construct great buildings, which were the marvel of their age. They turned their attention to the great questions of philosophy and the enigma of human life. As time went on, one city began to develop a reputation as the centre for the wisdom of the ancient world. It became a symbol for classical culture and learning. The city? Athens.

Athens began to rise to greatness under Pericles in the 5th century before Christ. It was at this stage in its history that many of the greatest buildings of the city were constructed. Alongside its military and political successes, the city became the home of some of the world's greatest philosophers. Socrates, Plato and Aristotle all made this city their home. After the death of Socrates in 399 BC, Plato left Athens, and travelled in Egypt, Sicily and Italy. In 387 BC, Plato returned to Athens to found the Athenian Academy. This took its name from its site, the 'grove of Academos'. It would go on to become the elite philosophical school that would dominate the thinking of the ancient world.

Plato can be said to have touched on most of the grand questions of philosophy in his writings. One of his most distinctive ideas is that there exists an independent world of 'Forms', which are the basis of all that we observe in the world. These include such ideals as Good, Truth and Beauty. Our ideas of what is good, true and beautiful are ultimately based upon these Forms. Plato treats the world of Forms as an independent world lying behind what we experience in everyday life. What we encounter in the world are copies, reflections or shadows of these ideals or Forms.

Plato developed this idea in one of the most famous literary analogies – the prisoners in a cave. Plato asks us to imagine a dark cave in which a group of people are chained so that they can only look in one direction. Behind them, a fire is burning and its light casts shadows on the wall of the cave. The prisoners can see nothing other than these shadows and so come to treat the shadows as the reality. Yet if they were freed from their chains, they could leave the cave and discover the real world. Before, they had only seen shadows of people and animals moving about; now they can see the real thing and realize that the shadows are only a dim copy of the reality to which they relate. An experience of the real world of light and colour would for ever eclipse the experiences of the dark cave, where flickering shadows were taken as reality.

The point that Plato was making is clear. The world in which we live is a world of shadows, a copy of the real world of Forms. The supreme task of philosophy is to allow us to escape from the cave – to experience a world which lies beyond it, which is seen in a dark, distorted and dim manner within the cave itself. The task of the philosopher is to break free from the limits of our world of experience, and somehow enter into the greater and more wonderful world that lies beyond it. But how?

Plato's quest for access to the world of Forms remains of supreme importance. His successors might state the problem in different ways, but the basic issues remain much the same. Is there a world beyond ours, which somehow makes its presence felt in and through our experience? Is the present world a copy of shadow of a greater, better and more beautiful world – and, if so, how can we gain access to this better world and enter into it? If we are to accept that we live in a dark cave, and have come to treat shadows as reality, how can we break free from the chains which bind us to that cave, and allow us to discover the world of light, colour and fragrance which lies beyond it? Is there life beyond the cave?

Yet alongside this quest for the ideal world, a darker theme may be discerned. Are we meant to gain access to this kingdom? Might we be like the Greek mythological figure of Prometheus who stole the fire of the gods? Might we intrude upon a forbidden world? Might we gatecrash a party to which we have not been invited, and find ourselves thrown out as unwelcome intruders? Or might we stumble across a divinity who did indeed create the world, but now wishes to be left undisturbed? Might we discover a jaded cosmic clockmaker, who now has no further interest in or concern for what was created?

And what might this better world be like? Might it be a hostile and abstract place, in which we are destined to wander in solitude, desperately seeking fulfilment? Paul Elmer Moore (1864–1937), one of America's greatest Platonist philosophers, had always been fascinated and deeply satisfied by the world of beautiful Platonic forms, the world of the purely ideal. But gradually, disillusionment set in. He began to experience a sense of what seemed to him to be an unutterable bleakness and solitariness. He was driven to search for something more – for a personal God – 'by the loneliness of an ideal world without a Lord'. He longed for those impersonal Platonic Forms to become personal – to turn into a face. 'My longing for some audible voice out of the infinite silence rose to a pitch of torture. To be satisfied I must see face to face; I must, as it were, handle and feel – and how should this be?'

Such concerns were

known long before Moore's time. Even in the first century of our era, many Athenians preferred to believe in the gods of ancient mythologies. These had a personal dimension to them, which was so clearly lacking in Plato's world of silent, abstract Forms. Yet there were hesitations. While many continued to affirm the classical pantheon – including Zeus and Hermes – others were anxious lest some additional, and hitherto unknown, God might be overlooked. Altars began to be erected with inscriptions to 'an unknown God'. The Epicureans and Stoics offered alternatives to Plato. So which was to be preferred? Athens was a city in turmoil, wondering whether God could, indeed, be known – and if so, how?

In was at this point that the apostle Paul arrived in Athens. During the period AD 53–55, Paul had been travelling along the northern coast of the Aegean Sea, speaking at cities such as Philippi and Berea. Finally, he moved on to speak at Athens, presumably travelling by sea for this final stage of the journey. Paul's preaching in the city stirred up considerable interest and controversy, and he was invited to explain his ideas to some of the citizens

Athens

of Athens, assembled at the Areopagus (Acts 17:22–34). The 'Areopagus address' is of enormous interest, as it opens up some of the questions we have been pondering in this chapter.

Paul affirms that there is indeed a God who has created this world. In particular, he has created humanity as his offspring in such a way 'that they would search for God, and perhaps grope for him and find him – though

ST PAUL PREACHING AT ATHENS, RAPHAEL (1483–1520)

indeed he is not far from each one of us' (Acts 17:27). Yet Paul does more than endorse the great tradition of humanity's quest for God; he insists that this God has made himself known by name. Referring to an altar he had noticed, dedicated 'to an unknown God', Paul declares: 'What therefore you worship as unknown, this I proclaim to you' (Acts 17:23). In other words, the divinity they were seeking, and to whom they had even managed to draw near, was a God who chose to make himself known.

What you worship as unknown, I proclaim to you. For Paul, we are not left on our own to discover God, nor yet to encounter a nameless and abstract force or ideal that we are obliged to call 'God'. Paul sets before the Athenians his vision of a personal God, who has made his name, character and purposes known to us. We are, according to Paul, dealing with a God who chooses to make himself available and accessible to us, who delights in knowing us and being known by him.

The idea that Paul develops, however briefly, in this address at the Areopagus is that of revelation. The fundamental theme is that God makes himself known to us. What nature suggests, God himself confirms. From a close study of the created world, we might well suspect that there is indeed a creator God, and that we will be restless until we know and embrace him. Yet this might be little more than a dream. How might such a suspicion be validated? How might our hunch that there is rather more to things than meets the eye be confirmed and eventually fulfilled?

For Paul, the answer is both simple and complicated. In its simple form, the answer can be found in the concluding words of his Areopagus address. Here, Paul speaks of God giving assurance concerning such ideas through raising Christ from the dead (Acts 17:31). For Paul, it is the person of Jesus Christ who is the ultimate ground of trusting in God and the promises that God makes to us. This theme is easy to set out; its exploration is rather more complicated. However, as it is so clearly important to Paul, we may follow it through and see where it takes us.

At first sight, it might seem curious, if not bizarre, to speak of any revelatory connection between God and Jesus Christ. Yet further reflection points to a certain inexorable logic to the suggestion. If God somehow is to be made known to us, the inhabitants of a world of time and space, God must somehow encounter us within the contours of that world. And if this happens, the entry of God into our world would transcend the accumulated wisdom of the ancients. It is a tantalizing thought. Might it be true?

So let us suppose, for the sake of argument, that there is a God. Suppose further that this God is not content simply to bring the universe into being and then withdraw from it – like a grumpy clockmaker who, having created a clock and wound it up, leaves it to run unattended. Imagine that we are dealing with a God who wants to make himself known to us. Suppose that the creation is indeed studded and spangled with hints of the nature and character of this God. Does not every artistic creation bear the sign of its maker and reflect something of the mind of that maker?

So how might such a God make himself known to us? How might we encounter such a God? We have been exploring the idea that God has made us to relate to him, and that we are unfulfilled until we do so. But might there not be another side to this coin? Might not God remain unfulfilled until we relate to him? Might this God therefore not passionately long to come and find us, even though we have probably wandered away from him? After all, some of the Gospel parables tell of the joy of people in finding what they had thought to be lost – the woman who finds a lost coin and the shepherd who tracks down a lost sheep, and carries it back to the safety of the sheepfold.

So how might God encounter us? How might God find us? Perhaps we can take a lead here from that parable of the lost sheep (Luke 15:3–7), which tells of a shepherd setting out to seek the wayward animal. There is no question of the shepherd expecting the sheep to find its own way back, or of calling the sheep in the hope that it will be able to return home unaided. The task demands that the shepherd goes to where the sheep is, in order to bring it home. If God is to encounter us, God must come to meet us where we are. And where are we? In a world of time and space. It is impossible for us to meet God where he is, as we are limited by the boundaries of our existence. It would therefore make a lot of sense if God were to enter the flux of human history, and find us there.

We find something very much like this in the Christian doctrine of the incarnation. The basic idea is that God stoops down to set foot in the sphere of our existence. Setting his glory and majesty to one side, God enters our history in human form, in the person of Jesus Christ. This idea is set out famously in the opening section of John's Gospel, which sets the coming of Jesus Christ against the panorama of cosmic history: 'the word became flesh and lived among us' (John 1:14). Rather than ask us to climb up a cosmic ladder in order to touch the face of God, God descends to us, to make his face known to us. To behold Jesus Christ is to gaze on the face of the God who lies behind this universe.

This may seem a presumptuous and ludicrously over-ambitious statement. If it is true, the importance of Jesus Christ lies in who he is, as much as in what he taught. In view of its importance, we may therefore move on to spend a little time trying to work out why Christians came to this conclusion and how it affects our outlook on things.

A Window of Perception

7

We have already noticed how Christianity places an enormous emphasis upon its central figure, Jesus Christ. But why is this? And how does it relate to the great human quest for wisdom and insight? An immediate answer to this question would go something like this. Jesus Christ is one of many moral teachers, standing in a long line of enlightened individuals who have tried to cast light on the mystery of life and how we should behave. We find these questions being addressed in the writings of ancient Israel, in the poetry of Homer, the tragedies of Euripides and the philosophical writings of Plato and Aristotle. The common human quest for meaning is also explored in the religious writings of Confucius, Lao-Tze, the Buddha and Mohammed. Jesus Christ therefore fits neatly into this pattern of human figures of wisdom.

Now we can easily agree that the New Testament depicts Jesus Christ as a teacher. The Gospels report that 'he taught with authority' and won the attention of the audiences in doing so. The Sermon on the Mount has been widely acclaimed as one of the finest pieces of moral and religious teaching to grace the face of this world. Its opening statements – widely known as 'the Beatitudes' – capture its tone well (Matthew 5:4–7):

> Blessed are those who mourn, for they will be comforted.
> Blessed are the meek, for they will inherit the earth.
> Blessed are those who hunger and thirst for righteousness, for they will be filled.
> Blessed are the merciful, for they will receive mercy.

In addition to such teachings, we find Jesus Christ using parables as ways of

THE SERMON ON THE MOUNT, JAMES JACQUES JOSEPH TISSOT (1836–1902)

conveying the central themes of his message concerning the kingdom of God. Each of these enigmatic sayings offers insights into the new values and lifestyles that Jesus Christ wished to introduce to humanity. An excellent example is provided by the parable of the Pearl of Great Price (Matthew 13:45–46):

> The kingdom of heaven is like a merchant in search of fine pearls; on finding one pearl of great value, he went and sold all that he had and bought it.

This parable sums up the eternal human quest for wisdom and fulfilment. The point is that the merchant, on finding a really valuable and beautiful pearl, realizes that all that he already owns pales into insignificance. Better to have one really precious and wonderful pearl than a collection of lesser valuables. He gladly sells all of these in order to possess something that is really worth having. In the same way, we all long for something in life that really satisfies. Along life's winding road we encounter many things that we initially think may be what we are looking for – only to find that they let us down. The kingdom of God is not like that, according to this parable. It is worth giving up everything to enter into this realm and dwell there in peace.

That parable in itself sums up the issue we have been exploring throughout this book. Where can we find this pearl of great price? How can we find something that will really satisfy us, rather than something that will temporarily check our hunger, before leaving us empty all over again?

The Christian answer to this question, as might be expected, has to do with Jesus Christ. But that answer is not quite what might be thought. The answer lies not primarily in what Jesus Christ taught – though that is viewed with the greatest respect – but in his identity. It is in knowing Jesus Christ that fulfilment is to be found, not simply appreciating and responding to his teaching about the values of the kingdom of heaven. We can see this point stated with great clarity in the writings of Paul, whose conversion to Christianity marked a turning point in the history of the church. Paul wrote these words: 'I regard everything as loss because of the surpassing value of knowing Christ Jesus my Lord' (Philippians 3:8). We can see this as a development of the parable we have just considered. Paul is affirming that, in his experience, everything that this world has to offer cannot compare with the privilege of knowing Jesus Christ.

Now where does this take us? Most obviously it places a very serious question mark against the popular view that Jesus Christ is yet another addition to a rather lengthy list of the religious and moral educators of humanity. It does not deny that his name belongs on that list; it does, however, compel us to ask whether this is anything even approaching an adequate account of his significance. To say that Jesus Christ is a great teacher could be compared to saying that a performance of Beethoven's Fifth Symphony is just an aggregate of vibrating air, or that a Van Gogh masterpiece is simply coloured mineral dust stuck on to a piece of canvas. These statements are true, as far as they go. But they do not go very far. They are only a small part of the truth and can be argued to be so inadequate that they mask, rather than reveal, the full significance of their subjects.

Perhaps the easiest way of appreciating this point is to read the New Testament, or look at the words of the great hymns or writings of the Christian church. They talk about 'being saved' through Christ, or 'being redeemed' through his death and resurrection. They speak of the identity of Jesus in terms of the 'Son of God' or 'Saviour'. And, perhaps most mysteriously, they use language about him being 'truly God and truly human' when they recite the Creeds in public worship. This seems a world away from the idea that Jesus Christ is a dispenser of moral wisdom.

This can be seen especially clearly when Christians talk about 'knowing Christ' – not just 'knowing about Christ', which might seem a more obvious way of speaking. This way of talking about Christ is not a new development; it is found firmly embedded in the New Testament, and has resonated with the Christian experience of Christ down the centuries. This manner of speaking is rich with meaning as it suggests that Christian faith is not an accumulation of factual information concerning Jesus Christ; it is

relational. This is puzzling, not least because it raises a very serious question: how can anyone 'know' someone who lived and died 2,000 years ago? Surely this way of speaking is inappropriate?

All of this is disconcerting to someone who is trying to make sense of Christianity. Such a person is like someone standing on the shore of a coral island, staring into the distance. She sees the ocean stretching ahead of her, with gently undulating waves caressing the shoreline. She perceives the

surface of the water as a series of ripples, unaware that beneath the surface is a living world of coral outcrops, richly populated with marine plants, and fishes darting colourfully in the sun-dappled sea. By focusing her attention on the surface, she has missed out on one of the wonders of the natural world.

So what lies beneath the surface of the Christian understanding of Jesus Christ? And why is it of such importance to the age-old human quest for significance and joy? There is no easy way of explaining this, other than to set out what Christians believe, and why, at this point. On the basis of a long and sustained reflection on the New Testament witness to Jesus Christ, linked with the personal experience of Christians in prayer and worship, the church set out its fundamental belief that Jesus Christ had to be thought of as 'truly divine and truly human'. This was seen as the only viable solution to the riddle of the identity of Christ. No human mystery novel has ever quite compared to the mystery of the identity of Christ.

So what factors compelled Christians to accept this conclusion? There is no space to set out these issues in the detail which they deserve. A sketch map must suffice, where a far more complex analysis is demanded. We may begin with an easy idea. The New Testament leaves us in no doubt that Jesus was a genuine human being. He was someone who felt pain, who wept over the death of his friend Lazarus and who knew what it was like to be hungry and thirsty. Yet this insight, on its own, is not enough to do justice to the rich biblical portrait of Jesus. We must move on to understand why.

The New Testament insists that Jesus was far more than a human being. Without in any way denying the real humanity of Jesus, the New

Testament applies words and titles to him that are reserved for God and attributes actions to him that are the privilege of God alone. Jesus claims to have authority to forgive sins – something which is the prerogative of God alone. New Testament writers use titles to refer to him that are laden with significance. For example, Jesus Christ is affirmed to be our 'Saviour' – again, doing something that only God is meant to do.

The Gospels also record the reactions of those who encounter Jesus Christ after his resurrection (a matter to which we shall return presently). One of those is Thomas, perhaps the most sceptical of the disciples. On finally being persuaded that Christ had indeed been raised from the dead, he responded with his own interpretation of the significance of Christ: 'my Lord and my God!' (John 20:28). Those disciples who were commanded by Christ to go into the world and 'make disciples of all nations' were overwhelmed by the presence of the risen Christ. Their response? 'When they saw him, they worshipped him' (Matthew 28:17). Yet only God is to be worshipped.

What are the implications of these telling straws in the wind, these mysterious clues to the identity of Jesus Christ? As Christians reflected on them, they came to the conclusion that Jesus Christ is not simply someone who does what only God can do – such as save his people and forgive their sins. He is able to do these things because of who he is. No other way of thinking or speaking about him seemed able to do justice to the biblical evidence. These conclusions are formalized in the Creeds of the Christian church, which affirm that Jesus is 'true God and true human being'. That statement does not resolve the mystery of the identity of Christ. It simply states what it believes to be the crux of the matter.

So why is this insight of such importance? Dorothy L. Sayers (1893–1957) put her finger precisely on the critical point at issue here: 'If Christ was only man, then he is entirely irrelevant to any thought about God; if he is only God, then he is entirely irrelevant to any experience of human life.' We can explore her point in two directions – negatively, in terms of what follows if the Creed is wrong at this point; and positively, in terms of what possibilities are opened up if it is right.

If the Creed is wrong, then Jesus is nothing more and nothing less than one of the great series of religious and moral teachers who have sought – generally without much success – to educate humanity. Any hints in the New Testament that Jesus Christ is more than this must be put down to wishful thinking, to misunderstandings, or perhaps even to blatant misrepresentation. If Jesus Christ is only a human being – no matter how splendid a specimen of humanity he may be – he is part of the problem, not its solution. He would have to reform the human race from within, whereas – as we shall see in the next chapter – it cries out for transformation from outside.

Suppose, again, that the Creed is wrong. If Jesus Christ were to speak to us about God, he would then speak to us as one who shares our condition of 'not being God'. He would speak with no greater authority than anyone else on the matter. God himself may speak authoritatively and reliably for God and about God. But anyone else must speak with a much lesser authority, as a second-hand witness. All the great teachers of the past would be on a level playing field, all equally distant from God in that none is God.

The Incredulity of St Thomas, Michelangelo Merisi da Caravaggio (1571–1610)

This is not the Christian understanding of Jesus Christ, and it is important to make this point unequivocally clear. This observation does not mean that the Christian position is right, nor does it mean that it is wrong.

NATIVITY WITH MUSIC-MAKING ANGELS ABOVE, GIOVANNI BATTISTA (1497–1555)

It simply means that the 'Jesus Christ as great teacher' model is not how Christians view things.

But suppose that the Creed is right. Suppose that Jesus Christ is indeed 'true God and true human being'. What might this have to say to us about his identity? What new possibilities does this disclose?

Perhaps the most important of these concerns our knowledge of God. God is made known to us, not as an abstract force or an impersonal being but as a personal reality. Jesus Christ is to be seen as the 'image of the invisible God' (Colossians 1:15). In other words, the invisible God is made known in the visible form of Jesus Christ – a historical person. We find this theme throughout the New Testament: to have seen Jesus Christ is to have seen God.

Jesus Christ is thus a window of perception, opening the way to fresh glimpses of the living God. Through this window, we perceive God as one who was willing to humble himself in order to restore us to fellowship with him. This theme of the humility of God is developed in many Christmas carols. Perhaps one of the finest and best-known statements of this theme of the self-humiliation of God is due to Mrs Cecil F. Alexander, in her carol 'Once in Royal David's City':

> He came down to earth from heaven,
>   who is God and Lord of all,
> and his shelter was a stable,
>   and his cradle was a stall;
> with the poor, and mean, and lowly
>   lived on earth our Saviour holy.

The window opened up upon the face of God by Jesus Christ allows us to see the creator God as one who willingly enters into his creation in order to bring us back to him. We are indeed made to relate to God – and God is prepared to do all that he can in order to bring about that relationship, fulfilling the deepest desires of the human heart. Having made us to long for him, God draws near to us so that we might be fulfilled and satisfied in him.

Taking this line of thought a little further, we can see what must be done if the deepest longings of the human soul are to be quenched and satisfied. We are made to relate to God; God has entered into history in order to fill the void within us. It remains only for us to allow him to enter in and fill that void. Perhaps it makes sense to think of the human soul as a great mansion, with many rooms – a favourite image of the Spanish writer Teresa of Avila (1515–82). The doors to that mansion and its many rooms must be opened before God may enter in and transform that cold and dark building with his warmth and radiance. We must throw aside any barriers that remain within us to the indwelling of God within our hearts. In one sense, faith can be thought of as saying 'Yes!' to God and throwing open the portals of our souls to the refreshing, renewing and transforming presence of the living God.

One of the issues here is the resurrection – the Christian affirmation that death was unable to hold Jesus Christ, who was raised by God from the dead and exalted to be at the right hand of God. There is a lot of technical language in that statement, which I cannot hope to unpack adequately in the space available. However, my concern here is to identify one of the consequences of this belief. If the resurrection did indeed happen, then encounter with Jesus Christ is not limited to any particularities of space or time. Saul of Tarsus met the risen Christ on the road to Damascus, and countless Christians since then have found it entirely natural to speak of encountering Christ in a similar way.

The resurrection also opens up another fascinating line of thought. Many are intrigued by what are often called 'near-death experiences'. These are visions of what lies beyond death, reported by individuals who have been close to death, yet have at the last moment pulled back and recovered from what would otherwise have been a fatal condition. Those visions often take the form of sensations of peace or joy, or a rapturous experience of a new land lying beyond anything hitherto known to humanity.

Yet there is a tantalizing difficulty here. Those who have provided such reports of what lies beyond death have not actually died. They have hovered close to that state, but have not entered it. Precisely because they were able to relay their experiences to others, they survived their brush, however close, with death. Perhaps they caught a glimpse of something real – but it was from a distance, perhaps too great a distance to allow their reports to carry the authority they would have liked.

But suppose someone really were to die. Suppose further that this is not the end of the story. Suppose this person were to rise from the dead. Would not such a person possess a unique authority to speak on the great themes of human nature and destiny? This thought-experiment can only hint at the importance of the resurrection and its implications for our thinking about the significance of Jesus Christ, and we must leave this intriguing matter there.

The Law of Nature

8

One of the most remarkable successes of the natural sciences has been their uncovering of the deep structure of the universe. Everything that happens within the universe seems to be governed by 'laws of nature'. One of Sir Isaac Newton's greatest achievements was to demonstrate that the same laws governed both the way in which an apple fell to earth from a tree and every aspect of the orbit of the planets and their moons. One single principle lay behind all of these observations. Newton's achievement in explaining the laws that governed the behaviour of planets, moons and apples was widely seen as the greatest intellectual achievements of his era.

The 'laws of nature' are not affected by the race, gender or social status of the observer. They are absolute and eternal. The ordering of the universe is objective, existing in reality and not merely in the mind of the beholder. And human reason seems able to uncover this ordering, setting it out in an intelligible manner. So how is all this to be accounted for? The Christian explanation is that they are grounded in the mind of God and expressed in the universe that has been created, bearing the divine imprint. Newton and other scientists of his day saw this regularity as reflecting God's work in creation. Robert Boyle spoke of God as the 'supreme and absolute Lord' of creation who 'established those rules of motion, and that order among things corporeal which we are wont to call the laws of nature'. For Newton, the sovereignty of God over the creation was to be expressed in terms of a divinely-imposed ordering and regularity within nature, which human reason could discern. Alexander Pope penned the following lines in praise of Newton's achievement:

Nature and Nature's Law lay hid in Night.
God said, let Newton be, and all was Light.

As astronomy became increasingly successful in predicting the movements of the planets in the late 16th and early 17th centuries, astronomers began to speculate on the reasons why mathematics was able to offer such convincing analysis of the known universe. The 16th-century astronomer

MASTER ISAAC NEWTON, ROBERT HANNAH (1812–1909)

Johann Kepler, who made huge advances in our understanding of planetary orbits, had no doubt that the reason for the success of mathematics lay in the creation of the world and the human mind by God:

> In that geometry is part of the divine mind from the origins of time, even from before the origins of time (for what is there in God that is not also from God?), it has provided God with the patterns for the creation of the world, and has been transferred to humanity with the image of God.

A similar point was made by Galileo Galilei, who attributed the success of his astronomical theories to mathematics being grounded in the being of God:

> Philosophy is written in this grand book, the universe, which stands continually open to our gaze. But the book cannot be understood unless one first learns to comprehend the language and read the letters in which it is composed. It is written in the language of mathematics.

The human body is also governed by the laws of nature. The way in which electrical impulses are transmitted by the central nervous system; the manner in which food is converted to energy through the digestive process; the way in which the human eye focuses on objects; and the manner in which the human limbs exert force – all conform to the laws of nature.

GALILEO GALILEI

Yet might there not be another form of ordering in the world, which has an important place in our reflections? Might there be a moral ordering of the universe, in addition to its physical ordering? The study of the universe reveals that it is ordered. Might there not be a moral order within this universe, flowing from the nature of the world as God's creation? Might there be something that is built into the fabric of the universe, and discerned – rather than imposed or constructed – by the human mind? Might not our minds be able to uncover this moral ordering?

This theme has been pursued since the dawn of civilization. We find it in Plato, and above all in the great Christian philosophers who held that there was an objective goodness which was grounded in the wisdom and character of God. And as that God also created humanity in his image, we have at least a limited ability to apprehend this good and to try to conform our lives to its pattern. 'Right' and 'wrong' are therefore not just human inventions. They are grounded on something much deeper, reflecting the will of God.

We have already seen how easily and naturally this notion emerges from the view that the world and humanity are created by the one and only God. There is a resonance between the created human mind and the pattern of its creator. The 'good' is something objective and eternal, rooted in the mind of God, yet capable of being grasped, at least in part, by obedient human reason.

Yet one of the greatest paradoxes of human nature is that we seem to prefer doing things that are wrong. They are somehow more interesting, more attractive, than those we know to be right. The great Roman poet Ovid put this rather nicely in his *Metamorphoses*:

> I see the better things, and approve; I follow the worse.

We often seem to see ourselves as exempt from the rules we would like others to respect. We may well have a strong sense of what is right – but we seem incapable of achieving it. The good things we would like to do somehow seem beyond us. So how can we achieve the good that is intended for us, if we cannot reach out and take hold of it?

The New Testament faces this issue head-on. Paul identifies this problem in his own experience, probably prior to his conversion, when he writes (Romans 7:18–19):

> I can will what is right, but I cannot do it. For I do not do the good I want, but the evil I do not want is what I do.

Paul speaks of being trapped, or being held captive, by a force that prevents him from achieving the good and binding him to a lower way of living. He recognizes the excellence of the 'law of God', yet is 'captive to the law of sin'. He is ensnared in his predicament. He wants to do good, yet finds himself being drawn down by some force or presence which frustrates his good intentions. He is unable to grasp the good on the one hand, or to resist evil on the other. So how can he get himself out of this apparently hopeless situation? Who could deliver him from this bondage?

Perhaps Paul's sense of despair here may seem a little overstated to some. Yet most will be able to identify with the predicament he describes. We have all made rash and hasty promises and found it impossible to keep them – like promising to be a nicer person, to give up those habits that some find distasteful or tedious, or to read six improving books a day. Sooner or later, reality intrudes into our dream world. We realize that we just cannot achieve our ambitious goals and become discouraged.

The same problem arises with evil. Somehow, we seem to desire something when the evocative word 'forbidden' is stamped upon it. As Mark Twain pointed out in *Pudd'nhead Wilson*, Adam 'did not want the apple for the apple's sake; he wanted it only because it was forbidden'. We feel the lure of the forbidden and are drawn to it, as moths are drawn to the flickering flame of a candle – even though it may end in our destruction.

It is as if there is an 'old Adam' within us, a force dragging us back to where we used to be, an inbuilt resistance to improvement, which pulls us down. We dream of excellence, yet achieve something rather less impressive.

Countless Christian writers have noted the strong resonance between the tragedy of common human experience at this point and the themes of the New Testament. We have the capacity to discern the good, but not, it seems, to achieve it. It is as if we are caught up in a tantalizing quest for something we long to possess, yet which seems to elude us. Like the great Quest for the Holy Grail, it is a noble yet forlorn yearning for something we believe to be worthwhile, yet sense lies beyond our grasp.

Augustine of Hippo (AD 354–430) was perhaps the most perceptive of the early Christian writers to deal with this theme, which he knew powerfully from his own experience. He spoke of sin as a force holding us captive, preventing us from ever grasping the presence of God, even though we had been created for precisely that purpose. Our longing to be possessed by God and to fulfil the good seem permanently thwarted and frustrated. We are trapped, like people in a deep hole in the ground. We may attempt to get out of it, but our pathetic scrabblings merely result in the hole getting deeper. We are ill, and need to be healed – but we cannot heal ourselves.

ST AUGUSTINE IN HIS CELL, SANDRO BOTTICELLI (1444/5–1510)

So what hope is there? For Augustine, we have been made to relate to God, and our hearts will be permanently restless until they finally find their rest in God. But if we cannot grasp the living presence of God, fulfilment lies beyond us. We simply seem unable to achieve our destiny in our own strength. Things seem to keep going wrong for us. If anything, our situation simply heightens our sense of emptiness. It is like a long-term prisoner who is offered his freedom. He begins to anticipate the joy of being at liberty, renewing friendships and fulfilling his cherished dreams. Yet the offer is then withdrawn, leaving the prisoner even more downhearted than before. There is nothing more devastating than having one's hopes raised, only to be dashed. We long for God, yet realize that this seems to be a doomed hope – if it could even be called a 'hope' at all.

At this point we must pause, and give careful thought to the Christian answer to this question. We may begin by looking at what Paul has to say when he brings his discussion of being trapped in his addiction to sin (Romans 7:24–25):

> Wretched man that I am! Who will rescue me from this body of death? Thanks be to God through Jesus Christ our Lord!

We see here a very simple statement of the Christian answer – that the death and resurrection of Jesus Christ somehow break down the human enslavement to sin, and make possible the new way of living and fulfilled existence that is God's intention for us. When Christians speak about such things as 'salvation' or 'redemption' in Christ, they are pointing to the transformation in our situation brought about by the coming of Christ into the world, and especially through his cross and resurrection.

So how, it may reasonably be asked, does this happen? Why do the death and resurrection of Christ have this impact? This is not an easy question to answer in the space available, and only the outlines of a full reply can be provided. Perhaps the most helpful way of beginning to reflect on this is to consider how we might think of the concept of sin.

Augustine of Hippo thought of sin as a disease, a condition of the human soul that inculcated a tendency to shy away from the good and embrace evil. The gospel, he suggested, was like a drug or a medical treatment that begins to heal us from our illness. In much the same way, he suggested that the church was like a hospital, a caring community in which the process of recovery and recuperation took place. Many Christian writers have found this imagery very helpful, seeing parallels with some great Old

Testament prophecies of healing through the suffering of an obedient servant of God. 'He has borne our infirmities and carried our diseases… upon him was the punishment that made us whole, and by his bruises we are healed' (Isaiah 53:4–5).

Anselm of Canterbury viewed sin as a moral deficiency within humanity, which required forgiveness. Sin was moral alienation from God that cut us off from a living relationship with God. Once that sin was forgiven, a relationship with God could be restored and the way opened to renewal and transformation. Again, this has proved a very fertile way of thinking about sin. Many theologians have pointed out how it takes up some Old Testament themes, e.g. 'Your iniquities have been barriers between you and your God, and your sins have hidden his face from you' (Isaiah 59:2). Forgiveness of sins opens the way to removal of this barrier.

Charles Wesley (1707–88) thought of sin in terms of being held captive, like a prisoner bound in iron fetters. The prisoner would be free only when those chains were snapped and the prison door thrown open. He set this out in his hymn 'Free Grace':

> Long my imprisoned Spirit lay,
>   fast bound in Sin and Nature's Night.
> Thine Eye diffused a quickening Ray;
>   I woke; the Dungeon flamed with Light.
> My Chains fell off, my Heart was free,
>   I rose, went forth, and followed Thee.

All these understandings of sin, however, share a common foundation. In some way, deliverance from sin is linked with the death of Christ on the cross. The New Testament affirms that this is so and deploys a rich range of images to illustrate the nature of the new life that results from this transformation. Yet it does not really offer us an explanation of precisely how and why this happens. It is enough, it seems, to know that this is so, without knowing exactly how or why it is so.

Yet theologians have not been slow to develop these hints of answers and to point out the inherent logic of the matter. They have developed theories that aim to offer an explanation of how Christ's death could achieve such results. These theories have real value, provided it is remembered that the theory is always secondary to the actuality. Christ's death achieves these things in advance of any theory we may develop concerning how it achieves them. This should come as little surprise. I can be healed of an infection by an antibiotic without understanding how it actually works. I just need to know what to do in order to benefit from it. In the same way, humanity was able to benefit from eating food for thousands of years before someone figured out the mechanism of our digestive processes.

So what theories might be offered? One that gained considerable influence in the 4th and 5th centuries based itself on the healing ministry of Jesus Christ. To be healed by Christ is to experience his healing touch. The incarnation thus brought our wounded humanity into contact with the healing divinity, leading to our renewal. 'What has not been assumed cannot be healed' (Gregory of Nazianzen).

A second approach holds that the cross represents a victory of God over the forces that oppress human nature – such as sin, death and evil. The cross can be seen as the point at which God engaged with the forces that trapped humanity, breaking their power over us. It was on the cross that God defeated and disarmed our enemies, opening the way for our salvation. A third sees sin as guilt, which needs to be washed away, leaving us as white as snow. Without forgiveness of our sins, we cannot hope to begin our lives anew.

Other approaches could easily be added. Yet ultimately, these are secondary matters. The great theme of the New Testament is that Christ's death upon the cross somehow holds the key to the perennial human struggle against meaninglessness and mortality. It is here that a new way of living is made possible and made available.

The question which then remains is whether we wish to accept and enter into this new way of life. For Paul, Christ's death and resurrection mean that eternal life is made available as a gift. What we could never attain has been gained for us and is offered to us as a gift. Yet, like any gift, we need to accept and receive it if we are to benefit from it in any way. The offer of a gift demonstrates the generosity of the giver; yet if we are to be enriched, we need to receive what is being offered. Faith is about recognizing our need for this gift that it is being offered to us and stretching out our hands to receive it.

9 The Great Anomaly

Every worldview has its weakness, its Achilles' heel. For the Christian, this point of vulnerability lies in the existence of pain and suffering within the creation. Is not this a fatal flaw that forces us to abandon Christianity, no matter what its attractions may be? How can anyone live with the tension created by the baleful presence of suffering in the world? In fact, things are not quite as straightforward as this simple account might suggest.

The natural sciences speak of 'inference to the best explanation'. When all is said and done, this basically means trying to work out which explanation of this complex and puzzling world seems to make the best sense of what we experience. Loose ends are to be expected; indeed, we would have every right to be suspicious of theories that seem to explain everything. Anomalies are accepted – indeed they are welcomed, in that they force further reflection on issues to ensure that no aspect of the theory has been left unexamined. Have all the observations been checked? And has the theory really been pushed to its limits, drawing on its full resources, in trying to explain what is observed?

The presence of suffering in the world is clearly an anomaly for those who believe in a good, loving and compassionate God. Is there not at least a serious tension here? For some, this is enough to compel them to abandon belief in such a God and any worldview that is linked to it. Yet it is not this simple. As philosophers of the natural sciences have never tired of pointing out, it takes far more than some disconfirming evidence to force the abandonment of a theory. Did the curious motion of Uranus force the abandonment of Newton's theories? Certainly not. It forced a critical examination of all the assumptions that had been made as part of those theories, until the flawed assumption was identified.

In this case, the defective assumption was that there was no planet in the solar system beyond Uranus. Once this assumption had been abandoned, the way was open to resolving the riddle of the movement of the planet Uranus within the boundaries of Newton's theories.

Did the failure of Darwin's theory of natural selection to explain many observed features of the natural world – by Darwin's own admission – force him to abandon this theory? No. He believed that the theory had a certain beauty, not to mention an ability to account for at least some of the more puzzling aspects of the natural world. Despite its difficulties, he believed that it would eventually be shown to be right. The grounds for trusting in the theory were, for Darwin, enough to allow him to stand by it, when faced with many apparent contradictions and a more than occasional lack of evidence for its assumptions.

That is what scientific theories are really like, and it is important to appreciate this point. As I discovered for myself back in the 1970s, working late into the night in Oxford University's research laboratories, it is far, far more difficult to confirm or refute a theory than might be expected. The natural scientist is perfectly prepared to live with a tension between the 'now' and the 'not yet' – the 'now' of a good theory, which explains much but not all, and is confronted with difficulties and anomalies, and the 'not yet' of the day when the theory will finally be verified, either by being developed to take account of these difficulties, or by the difficulties in question being shown not to be as important as was once thought.

Now how do these musings relate to the issue of suffering? The general principles which relate to any attempt to make sense of the complex world of experience must be held to apply to this problem as well. The reality of suffering is clearly a difficulty for the Christian worldview. It does not, however, compel the abandonment of that worldview. Reality is just too fuzzy and muddled for such a drastic initial step. Instead, we must recognize that theories of life do coexist with riddles, puzzles and anomalies, and aim to explore the matter more deeply. Might a Christian perspective have greater explanatory potential than at first we thought?

Adam and Eve, Lucas Cranach the Elder (1472–1553)

The first point that might be made here is that the world is not the way it is meant to be. It is like a beautiful city, ravaged by war. It is like a building, built to encourage joy and peace, that has been turned into a place of cruelty and pain – like some of the beautiful monasteries of the Gulag Archipelago, which were turned into Soviet labour camps under Stalin. What had been created for peace and reflection was debased and scarred, being reduced to a place of despair and torment. God brought the world into being as a place of repose and delight, a garden in which we might find peace and closeness to our creator. Yet the garden has become a wilderness, just as the beautiful city has become a ruin inhabited by jackals. This is not how things are meant to be.

Christian theology uses the language of 'fallenness' to describe this state of affairs. The world has fallen away from its God-given goals. All kinds of things have crept into the world to deflect it from its original purpose. We must never draw the conclusion that the world as we know it is the world as it ought to be. This is a good world that has gone wrong, yet which retains the memory of what it once was and the hope of what it finally will become. It is like a country that has been invaded by an occupying force, which recalls its days of freedom in the past and eagerly awaits its liberation in the future.

There is no denying the presence of suffering now. Yet this is not what was intended, nor how things shall remain. One of the threads that can be disentangled from the great Christian tapestry of redemption is that of restoration. In some way, redemption restores God's good creation to what it was meant to be. Redemption is about re-creation, a recapturing of the lost innocence and joy of God's intentions for his world. Though pain and suffering are part of the fabric of this present order, it is an order that will pass away and be displaced by a new creation. Pain, suffering, death and sorrow will have no place in the New Jerusalem. We live in the hope of the final elimination of the forces that cause us such grief. Christians will therefore live with the tension generated by pain and sorrow in their lives and thoughts, while affirming that this is a characteristic of this transient order that will one day give way to a restored and renewed creation.

A present tension is thus counterbalanced by a future hope – by the expectation that the future will resolve what is at present an enigma. We see darkly, as through a mirror, at present; then we shall see things as they really are. This might at first seem to be special pleading, taking refuge in the notion of future verification of a present anomaly. Yet this is far more common than might be thought, as can be seen from a classic example in the history of science.

Einstein's general theory of relativity was one of the most ambitious and exciting intellectual developments of the first decades of the 20th century. If it was correct, Einstein declared, it predicted three important observable consequences. First, it offered a highly accurate explanation of what is usually known as 'the anomalous precession' of the planet Mercury. This had been known since about 1865, but had never been accounted for. Second, it predicted that a beam of light would be deflected on account of the gravitational mass of the sun. The extent of this deflection could be very accurately calculated and within 10 years it was shown that Einstein's theory corresponded superbly with the latest experimental findings.

ALBERT EINSTEIN

There, was however, a third prediction. Einstein argued that the gravity of the sun would have an impact on the light emitted from its orb. This 'gravitational redshift' was due to the reduction of the velocity of light by the mass of the sun. But the extent of this reduction was infinitesimally small – 2.12 parts in a million. So minute was this effect that it simply could not be detected by any technique available in the 1920s.

So what was to be done? Einstein's theory seemed elegant and achieved an impressive degree of success in terms of its explanation of what could be experienced of the world. But one of its predictions could not be confirmed. Perhaps Einstein was wrong and his theory would have to be abandoned. Yet most did not think so. They believed that his theory was sufficiently persuasive to allow them to trust that, at some point in the distant future, final confirmation of its predictions would take place. In the meantime, they were perfectly prepared to live with this unresolved tension. They lived and thought as if Einstein's theory was true, even though they knew that only a future generation would know whether this was properly warranted or not. What they knew seemed good enough to them. They would trust that Einstein was right, and allow a future generation the luxury of knowing that he was.

In the event, the third prediction was confirmed in the 1960s, a generation later, when a new spectroscopic technique became available capable of observing the predicted effect. Yet nobody was entirely surprised. Nobody seems to have suspended belief in Einstein's theory of relativity until this final confirmation came through.

So what is the relevance of this famous incident in the history of science to our reflections? It shows that we can put our trust in a theory without having final confirmation of its truth. A theory can be good enough to gain our trust, even though some of its predictions and promises lie in the future.

There is a second point of importance. We sense that there is something wrong about pain and suffering. We don't get to that point by a reasoned argument. There's something deeper there – something within us that cries out 'this can't be right!' But why is this? If nature is just an accident, the result of blind natural forces, we should not be unduly disturbed by the presence of pain and suffering. It would just be the inevitable outcome of a pointless world, yet another meaningless aspect of a meaningless world.

Yet we do feel that suffering is wrong. There is a paradox here, in that we already seem to have an idea of how things ought to be. It is as if we have an inbuilt sense of the way the world was meant to be, and feel the pain of suffering with especial force because it seems to contradict our expectations. For the Christian, this makes sense. We have a deeply ingrained notion of the character of God and hence what anything that derives from God ought to be like. If we sense that the universe is unjust, we must have a notion of what a just universe would be like. As we have seen, it is possible to argue that the consonance between God, the world and ourselves, resulting from the doctrine of creation, is such that we should expect a degree of correspondence, however slight, between our minds and the mind of God. Grasping at least something of what the notion of 'justness' means, we sense that the present state of things is unjust.

So what does this mean? For the Christian, the answer lies in the memory of the way things were and the hope of the way things shall be. This strong sense that suffering is a scandal rests on our realization of what God intends the world to be. We recognize the disparity between what we experience and what we know ought to be the case. This brings home to us that the present world is not our true home – that it is a 'vale of soul-making' (John Keats), not our permanent residence. We are passing through, on our way to a true homeland, in which suffering will no longer be with us.

Yet the full Christian answer to the enigma of suffering does not lie in reflecting on God but in reflecting on the person of Jesus Christ. Why? Many answers might be given. The simplest might go like this. Jesus Christ suffered death by a protracted and painful death – crucifixion. Everything that we know about this form of public execution sends a shiver down our spines. Designed to humiliate as much as to punish with pain, crucifixion inflicted suffering like no other punishment of the ancient world. If ever a human being suffered, Jesus Christ did. We can therefore take at least some comfort in knowing that someone else has suffered like us – perhaps even more so.

Yet the full Christian answer goes far deeper than this. We are not talking simply about a solidarity of suffering, in which Jesus Christ throws in his lot with the common suffering and pain of the human race down the ages. While this is true, it does not go to the heart of the Christian understanding of the significance of Jesus Christ. Suppose – just suppose – that the traditional Christian understanding of Jesus Christ as 'truly God and truly human' is right. We have seen some of the reasons that might be given for this assertion. What if this were true? What difference might it make?

The implication is immediate. God knows suffering. The God who created the world knows and shares in its suffering. God has already entered into the value of suffering that we call 'history', and borne its costly and baleful weight. God stepped into a fallen world, and suffered its pain and agony. As we have seen, Jesus Christ is no messenger, sent to bring back reports of the state of the world to its creator. In Jesus Christ, God entered into that world, experiencing its tragedy and pain at first hand.

When I was young, I recall reading a fairy tale. I cannot remember much about it, except that its general drift went like this. There was once a good king, who loved his people very much – but never actually got to meet them. He lived in his glittering palace, enjoying the many privileges of his rank and was shielded by his well-meaning courtiers from the hardships and sorrows of his people. He was, however, determined to find out what it was really like in the world outside his palace. He therefore disguised himself as a peasant and slipped out of his palace at dead of night. He would live in the world as one of its ordinary inhabitants, coming to know it for himself, rather than having to rely on the heavily doctored reports of others. When he returned to his palace, it was as a wiser and better man. He now knew what his people were suffering. He would be a more compassionate king from now on.

I do not mean to suggest that the incarnation can be directly paralleled by this charming story. But I think there is a point being made that is of supreme importance to the theme of suffering. We are not dealing with a God who looks down on humanity in a detached manner, like the great

Olympian deities of the ancient world. Rather, we come to know a God who is passionately concerned with those whom he brought into being, and longs to share their sorrows and finally bring them to a kingdom from which suffering, pain and tears have been banished. We are able to take great comfort from knowing that this God is indeed compassionate and that this compassion is expressed in action, not merely in words.

So much did this God care for his suffering people that he entered into their world, setting to one side those divine prerogatives that might exempt him from suffering and pain. The one who need not suffer chose to do so, taking the pain of the world upon his shoulders, as Atlas is said to have borne the weight of the world upon his. Through his sufferings as God incarnate, Jesus Christ threw open the doors of the New Jerusalem – a city in which suffering is no more (Revelation 21:4). Before Jesus Christ, people suffered with dignity – as with Socrates, who committed suicide in a noble and dignified manner. Yet after Jesus Christ, people can suffer in hope, knowing that there lies ahead a homeland from which this enemy has been banished.

10 Doctrine Rears its Ugly Head

The human appetite for wonder is raised to new heights by some of the great sights of the natural world. Nature at its most beautiful evokes a sense of awe within us – a sense of beauty that sometimes leaves us breathless. Many of the greatest poets have been exhilarated by the glories of nature – such as William Wordsworth (1770–1850), who found himself thrilled at the unexpected sight of a vast expanse of daffodils in the English Lake District, or electrified by the sudden appearance of a rainbow during a storm:

> My heart leaps up when I behold
>   a rainbow in the sky.

Others have been held captive in wonder by the spectacle of a glorious sunset, a mountain range delicately shrouded in mist, or the steady glow of the stars of the sky at night.

Yet all natural phenomena, whether they move us to ecstasy or disgust, can be explained and accounted for by natural principles. This has alarmed the poets, who see such scientific theories as robbing the natural world of much of its wonder. In his 1820 poem 'Lamia', John Keats (1795–1821) complains of the effect of reducing the beautiful and awesome phenomena of nature to the basics of scientific theory. The theory may help us understand them – but somehow, it seems to deprive them of their glory. Keats here expresses a widely held concern: that reducing nature to scientific theories empties nature of its beauty and mystery, and reduces it to something cold, clinical and abstract:

Do not all charms fly
at the mere touch of cold philosophy?
There was an awful rainbow once in heaven:
we know her woof, her texture; she is given
in the dull catalogue of common things.
Philosophy will clip an Angel's wings.

Keats uses the idea of 'unweaving the rainbow' to express his concern. Does not the scientific explanation of the colours of the rainbow in terms of refraction of light through raindrops somehow destroy any sense of awe or amazement at this arc in the sky?

In one sense, Keats is right. Most who turn from the contemplation of a great natural spectacle to a scientific textbook, there to read the phenomenon described and analysed in neat little formulae, will feel that they have somehow turned away from something real and wonderful to something less real and considerably less satisfying. Yet Keats is not entirely right. The scientific theories which account for our observations of nature often have a beauty in themselves, especially when they are expressed mathematically. Beauty lies in the eye of the beholder and there are many who find the elegance of precise scientific theories to be at least as inspiring as the natural events to which they relate.

A similar situation exists in the case of Christian doctrines. Many find themselves puzzled by these, wondering why they should be necessary. They may have been out in the Arabian desert late at night, and found themselves overwhelmed by a sense of the presence of God amidst the stillness and silence of the endless sands. How can the terse statements of the Creeds ever do justice to that sense of the immensity and vastness of God? Do they not demean or devalue him? Or they read the Gospel accounts of the ministry and encounters of Jesus Christ and find in these narratives something compelling and authentic. They read, for example, of the encounter of Christ with the Samaritan woman at the well (John 4), in which the woman's perception of the situation undergoes a dramatic change. She initially sees a thirsty and tired man, exhausted from a hot day's journey. As they converse, she comes to realize that here is someone who is able to quench the deeper thirst that lies within her and everyone she knows – someone who himself is the source of a living spring of water, leading to eternal life.

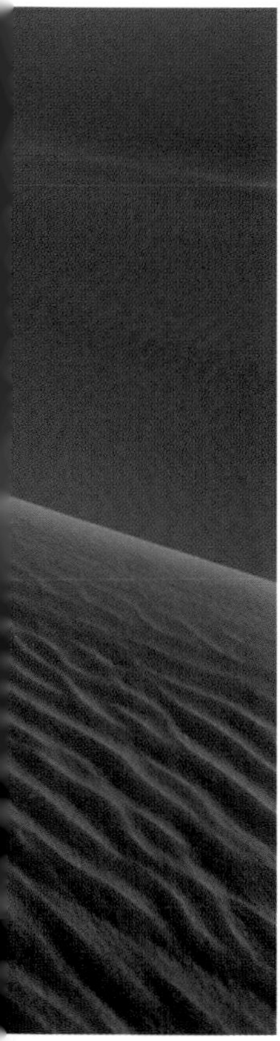

To turn from these Gospel narratives to the formulae we find in the Creeds of the church – which affirm, for example, that Jesus Christ is 'consubstantial with the

Father' – causes many to feel that they are turning away from a living, dynamic and compelling person to something that is dull, pedantic and petty. We are bombarded by an artillery of theological words, where we would much prefer to touch the face of God, or enter the gates of the New Jerusalem. There has never been any lack of people who feel that doctrine represents the pedantic side of faith – an aspect of Christianity which could profitably be dispensed with. What would be lost if such neat and tidy little formulae were to be abandoned?

These are fair and important questions and they must be taken seriously. To begin with, we need to note that Christianity makes an appeal to the mind, the imagination and the emotions. We may explore each of these briefly.

First, Christianity makes sense; it makes an appeal to the mind. It has a rationality which is real, though often difficult to grasp fully from outside the perspective of faith. As Augustine of Hippo once remarked, 'unless you believe you will never understand'. One of the great themes of the Christian faith down the ages is that, once grasped, the full intellectual richness and resilience of the faith can be appreciated. This is often expressed in a Latin tag associated with the 11th-century writer Anselm of Canterbury: *fides quaerens intellectum*, 'faith seeking understanding'.

Yet Christianity also appeals to the imagination. Reading the Gospel narratives helps us to generate a mental picture of what is taking place. We linger lovingly over the words and phrases of the text, as we allow them to trigger off a cascade of images, bringing a new depth and quality to our thinking. We know the story of Christ properly only when we allow our imaginations to play out its chapters in the theatre of our minds, and see things happening as if we were present to witness them for ourselves. It is no accident that many of the greatest artists have found the Gospels to be a rich source of inspiration for their works of art – which can in turn become a means of further enhancing our appreciation of the Gospel passages we are reading and thinking about.

Christianity also involves an engagement with the emotions. The most obvious instance of this would be the Gospel narratives of the crucifixion, which depict the pain and humiliation experienced by Christ on the cross. It is very difficult to read these accounts without being deeply moved, perhaps moved to tears. Once more, this has proved a powerful theme for artists and musicians – for example, J.S. Bach's passion chorales, which use evocative music to accompany the Gospel accounts of Christ's suffering, death and burial. We are, I think, meant to be moved emotionally by these and other sections of the New Testament, and we will have failed to have engaged with them fully and properly if this were not so.

Some people will place the emphasis upon one of these aspects, others upon another. They are all, however, integral to any serious engagement with the reality of God. To affirm one is not to deny another; it is to see it in another perspective, to approach it from another direction. It might reasonably be suggested that there is a danger of a skewed reading of the matter here. It is easy to imagine someone adopting a purely intellectual approach to Christianity, ignoring its emotional aspects. Others might react against what they would see as a rather cold, detached and cerebral viewpoint, and insist that the place of joy and other emotions should be fully recognized.

Doctrines make their appeal to the mind; they are an integral aspect of any attempt to understand the Christian faith. They are not, and were never meant to be, a substitute for the living witness of the New Testament to Christ, or the Christian experience of the presence of God in our lives. Rather, doctrines are a framework that give strength to these matters. They can be thought of as serving two functions. Positively, they set out the inner spiritual dynamic of the Christian faith. They establish links between different aspects of that faith and show clearly how it possesses a remarkable intellectual coherence. Negatively, they guard against misunderstandings of the faith.

The main role that doctrine plays is positive. It is like a scientific explanation of a rainbow. It is not meant to replace the awe-inspiring natural event, but to deepen our understanding of what is actually going on. Nature evokes awe; theory evokes cognition. The same general pattern is encountered when dealing with doctrines. The person of Jesus Christ gives rise to wonder; doctrines about Jesus Christ give rise to understanding. Doctrines tie together the many biblical strands of witness to God and to Christ, integrating their insights into a coherent vision of reality.

Second, doctrines have a defensive role. They are like fences enclosing the pastureland of the New Testament, ensuring that its witness to the significance of Jesus Christ is protected and safeguarded. Often, the main threat to Christianity is nothing more serious than common sense, which, for example, baulks at the idea that Jesus Christ can be 'truly God and truly human' or that – to mention a topic that everyone has urged me to avoid on account of its difficulty! – God is a trinity. Now common sense is like a watchdog, which barks when it smells a rat. Precisely because these doctrines are unusual, they need to be justified. It is important to demonstrate why Christianity came to the conclusion that these were right, just as it is equally important to resist the idea that common sense is always right!

To give an example. The common-sense view of things is that Jesus Christ is basically like the rest of us human beings. He may be holier, nicer and better than most of us – but he is unquestionably in the same ball park as us. Now it is easy to understand where this is coming from, and it must be respected as a genuine expression of anxiety and puzzlement over the Christian insistence that Jesus Christ is actually rather more than that. But this does not amount to the refutation of the Christian view; rather, it can be seen as a respectful request to explain why this common-sense view is not adequate.

As we have already devoted attention to this question earlier in this book, it would be appropriate to explore this general issue by looking at another area of Christian doctrine at which common sense begins to bridle at the apparent absurdity of what the church believes. So what better example of apparent lunacy to explore than the doctrine of the Trinity?

For many Christians, the idea that there is 'one God in three persons'

The Trinity, Jacopo di Cione (active 1362, died 1398/1400)

is difficult to grasp and seems to make a simple gospel needlessly complicated. Common sense, it might seem, is much more reliable here. Why not just speak of a God out there and have done with it? Why introduce all these baffling ideas about a 'Trinity'?

The basic Christian answer to this question takes the following form. The common-sense view of God may be admirably economical and simple. But it asks us to believe in a distant and remote God, who may once have created the world but has no further interest in it. This God cannot redeem us or enter into our history in order to meet us. It is not the God we read about in the Old or New Testaments and it is not the God whom Christians experience in prayer and worship. In short: the God of common sense cannot be identified with the God of Christianity. The doctrine of the Trinity therefore aims to distinguish the God that Christians believe in from the rival divinity suggested by common sense.

The Christian experience of God is immensely rich. It is vitally important to do justice to the distinctiveness of this God, even if the result seems difficult to understand at times. The basic themes that must be included in any basic account of the Christian God are, by general assent:

✤ This God is the one who created the world, and all that is in it.

✤ This God redeemed the world in Christ.

✤ This God is present with us now in his Spirit.

It might make things much simpler if we reduced our vision of God to just one of these elements. For example, we might suggest that it is good enough to believe in God as our creator. But this would be to deny that God redeems us, or that he cares for us. It is unquestionably easier to believe. Yet it is actually a radically impoverished view of God and arguably not a Christian view of God at all.

For the Christian, it is essential to do justice to the way God actually is known, rather than reducing God to a level at which we can understand him. The doctrine of the Trinity summarizes the greatness of God, partly by reminding us of all that God has done. It encourages us to broaden our vision of God. Above all, it demands that we do not falsely limit God by insisting that he fits into our limited understanding. The Greek philosopher Protagoras argued that 'humanity is the measure of all things'. Yet how can we allow God to be limited by the vagaries of a frail and finite human reason?

Patrick, the patron saint of my native Ireland, sets out a vision of God in the great hymn generally known as 'St Patrick's Breastplate'. This hymn sets out the richness and the depth of the Christian understanding of God. The hymn begins by surveying the vast panorama of the works of God in creation – one of the great themes of Celtic Christianity. The wonders of nature are reminders that God's presence and power undergirds the world of nature:

> I bind unto myself today
> the virtues of the star-lit heaven,
> the glorious sun's life-giving ray,
> the whiteness of the moon at even,
> the flashing of the lightning free,
> the whirling wind's tempestuous shocks,
> the stable earth, the deep salt sea,
> around the old eternal rocks.

The hymn then turns its attention to the work of God in redemption. It declares that the same God who created the world – the earth, the sea, the sun, moon and stars – acted in Jesus Christ to redeem us:

> I bind this day to me for ever,
> by power of faith, Christ's incarnation;
> his baptism in Jordan river;
> his death on Cross for my salvation;

his bursting from the spicèd tomb;
  his riding up the heavenly way;
his coming at the day of doom;
  I bind unto myself today.

We are thus invited to reflect upon the history of Jesus Christ: his incarnation, baptism, death, resurrection, ascension and final coming on the last day. These powerful ideas do not displace the belief that God created the world, and may be discerned in its wonders; it supplements this, by focusing on another area of the power and activity of God. All these, Patrick affirms, are the action of the same God who created us and redeems us through Jesus Christ.

Yet the hymn has not quite finished; there is another aspect of the activity and presence of God to be surveyed. Again, this is not to be seen as an alternative or substitute for what is already believed; it rounds off the full and authentic Christian vision of the character and power of God. The same God who called the universe into being and redeemed us through Jesus Christ is also the God who is present with us here and now:

I bind unto myself today
  the power of God to hold and lead,
his eye to watch, his might to stay,
  his ear to hearken to my need.
The wisdom of my God to teach,
  his hand to guide, his shield to ward;
the word of God to give me speech,
  his heavenly host to be my guard.

The hymn thus affirms that the one and the same God created the world, entered into our world and redeemed us in Christ, and is present as a living reality at this present moment. No other account of the nature and activity of God is adequate to do justice to the Christian witness to God, and no other doctrine of God can therefore be thought of as 'Christian'.

So why have doctrines about God? In order to safeguard God's glory, beauty and majesty, and avoid allowing debased and diluted concepts of God to pass themselves off as authentically Christian. It is like a manufacturer who develops a way of making very high quality glassware. Rival manufacturers flood the market with cheap imitations, which look something like the original but are of much lower quality. In an effort to protect the market from these cheap imitations, the original manufacturer trademarks a name for this glassware. From now on, nobody can use this name; it refers to the high quality product alone. To buy glassware going by this name is to be assured of its origination and quality.

The doctrine of the Trinity can be thought of as trademarking the Christian view of God. It is not the same as the 'common-sense' view of God, nor is it the same as the Islamic view of God. This is neither a criticism nor commendation of the Christian view; it is simply stating that the Christian conception of God is distinct, and that the preservation of this distinctiveness is essential to the Christian faith and those who wish to learn about it.

Doctrine, then, is inevitable and proper. It must raise what seems to some to be its ugly head, because it is already implied in what we believe about things. Yet the doctrines cannot be thought of as a substitute for the reality to which they refer. Doctrines are like signposts, enabling us to discover the full reality to which they point. We love God, not doctrines; we encounter God as a living personal reality, not some words on a piece of paper. Doctrines are like maps that show how things relate to each other, and help us see what we must do to discover and encounter the God whose presence we discern within the world of nature. Life is a journey; that map helps us work out where we are and what our options are. And people who are journeying need that map if they are to reach their final destination.

So important is this final point that we may move on to explore it in greater detail in the following chapter.

11 THE END OF OUR JOURNEY

Whether we like it or not, we have all embarked on a voyage which we call life. We had no choice in the matter. It is something that is presented to us as a given. Indeed, the very fact that we are able to reflect on the meaning of life is a direct consequence of that journey being under way, wherever it may take us. Life, for some, is a series of happenstances and accidents, which leads from birth to death with the dreadful predictability of a political speech. Perhaps it is all meaningless. Perhaps life leads to death as inevitably as the fruit borne by a tree finally drops to the ground. D.H. Lawrence (1885–1930) saw the falling of this fruit as a melancholy reminder of the inevitability of death:

> Now it is autumn and the falling fruit
>   and the long journey towards oblivion –
> have you built your ship of death, O have you?
>   O build your ship of death, for you will need it.

Yet who really knows? Just about everyone who is anyone has thought and written about it – and the sum total of their thoughts can hardly be said to represent a consensus. Some see life as totally pointless and recommend that we make the best of it. Others see life as having a real goal and purpose (though they are far from agreed as to what this is) and urge us to discover this. But who can say whether life has any real meaning or not? To do that, we would need to rise above the course of human existence, and survey it from outside the flux of our human situation. That is the view from nowhere, precisely because nobody occupies that privileged vantage position. Perhaps God might have some ideas on the matter, as he is supposed to occupy that kind of position.

Yet in that throw-away line there lies a nugget of truth which might well be the most important discovery that anyone could ever hope to make. Suppose that there is a God who brought us into existence for a purpose? In other words, imagine not simply that there is a God but that there is a God who has a definite objective in mind for us – that, in creating us, he created us for a purpose, and that this God longs to achieve that purpose in and for us. And there are clues to this within the world we know and experience. Even though do not have direct access to the grand vision of reality, what we know seems to point to something real and significant lying beyond the horizons of the known.

It is like looking at a section of a map. Somewhere off the map there lies a town. Yet the existence of that town is suggested by what we see on the section of the map that we do possess. We can see roads leading off the map that look as if they might converge. And where else might they converge, other than at a town? We cannot see the full picture, but what we can see points to there being a town nearby. There are clues embedded within the world that we do know concerning that which we do not – yet.

The world around us and our own thoughts and longings offer us clues to our purpose. We possess a sense of longing for something that seems to lie beyond the created order, yet is somehow signposted by the creation. Yet how reliable are these? Have we misread them? Have we invested these hints and clues with our own misguided hopes when in fact they might mean something else – or nothing at all?

It is for this reason that the Christian doctrine of the incarnation is so important. Taken on its own, the witness of the created order is ultimately ambivalent. Yet taken along with the pattern of divine activity and presence that we find in Jesus Christ, we can discern a consistent and coherent pattern. We are dealing with a God who has created us to relate to him, who has left his distinctive mark upon the universe and upon our minds, and who has entered into our history in order to bring us home to him. This, in sum, is the Christian view of human nature and destiny. This way of speaking immediately suggests the image of a map. A map allows us to impose order and structure upon a landscape, enabling us to undertake our journey. So what kind of map are we talking about?

The framework that Christianity offers us for making sense of the journey of life is complex and rich. Its central theme is that this world is not our final destiny. It is not where we ultimately belong. We are indeed born into this world but our true hope and goals lie elsewhere. We are in exile, and long to return to our homeland – a homeland whose presence we sense and whose enticement we feel. We are offered the citizenship of heaven, so that we may return there, not as intruders or invaders, but as welcome and honoured guests.

This image of an 'exile' needs careful unpacking as it holds the key to a right understanding of our situation. The imagery is grounded in the history of the people of Israel, and especially the catastrophic events which accompanied the fall of Jerusalem to the Babylonian empire in the 6th century before Christ. Many of the inhabitants of the fallen city were deported to Babylon, where they would remain. Their only hope of return was the defeat of Babylon by a still greater imperial power. Yet at the time this seemed a forlorn hope.

In the event, a great act of liberation took place. The Persian empire rose to power under Cyrus and finally overthrew Babylon. As a result, the people of Jerusalem were liberated from their captivity in Babylon and allowed to return home to Jerusalem – the homeland that many had never dreamed they would see again. The way home through the wilderness was long and difficult – but the thought of returning home quickened the steps and raised the spirits of the returning exiles.

Exile is about absence from where the heart belongs. While living in exile in Babylon, the people of Jerusalem longed to return to their homeland. Their hearts ached for their native land. This deep sense of longing for Jerusalem can be seen in many of the writings of this period, such as Psalm 137:

By the rivers of Babylon –
  there we sat down and there we wept
  when we remembered Zion…
Let my tongue cling to the roof of my mouth
  if I do not remember you,
  if I do not set Jerusalem above my highest joy.

Returning to Jerusalem was the most important thing in the world for these pathetic exiles. They lived in Babylon but their hearts were in Jerusalem. The hope of return was what kept them going. They sang the songs of Zion in that strange land to keep their memories and their hopes alive. This was not where they belonged.

We could explore the same theme with reference to Plato's cave, which we considered earlier (chapter 6). In his dialogue *The Republic*, Plato asks us to envisage a group of people who are chained in a dark cave, so that they can only see a world of flickering shadows, cast by a fire. The business of the real world takes place nearby, and its shadows are thrown up on the cave wall. The people in the cave have no idea that there is another world, beyond the cave. They know only that dark, smoke-filled and damp place of exile and bondage. If someone were to tell them that there existed a land of light, colour and sound, they would find the thought impossible to take in.

Yet that is where we are. We live in a world which we believe to be the only reality. Yet there is a world beyond that cave, which is our true homeland. Hints of that world beyond have reached us, even in the cave. More than that; someone has come to us from the world beyond, to affirm that it exists, to convey its wonder to us and to enable us to enter into its joys and delight.

This way of thinking allows us to construct a map, setting out our journey. We could think of ourselves as being like the people of Jerusalem,

JERUSALEM

exiled in Babylon. Where they are is their place of exile; where they want to be is their homeland, Jerusalem. Our journey of life is thus about travelling home, from Babylon through the great wildernesses back to Jerusalem. The liberation of the people of Jerusalem by Cyrus can be seen as a 'type' or anticipation of our own liberation from sin by Christ's death upon the cross. And our homeland? The New Jerusalem, which awaits us. We can therefore see life in terms of a definite framework. We are in a place of exile and we are travelling to our homeland. We can live in hope, knowing that we shall one day arrive at the New Jerusalem and be welcomed within.

We find this framework developed at several points in the New Testament. When writing to the church at Philippi, Paul took advantage of the fact that the city was a Roman colony to develop a powerful image of the Christian hope. Roman citizens had the right of return to Rome after serving overseas. During their term of service in the colonies, they could look forward to the day when they would return home. Philippi is their place of temporary exile, but Rome is their home. In moments of loneliness and

homesickness, the Romans in that city could console themselves with memories of the eternal city and anticipate the day when they would travel home. Paul therefore reassured the Christians at Philippi that their 'citizenship is in heaven' (Philippians 3:20). They have the right to return there and the right to dwell there. It is their homeland.

Such themes have been explored throughout Christian history. In his 'Prayer to Christ', Anselm of Canterbury (1033–1109) explores the significance of his longing to be with Christ in heaven. The thought of being with Christ simultaneously heightens his sense of sadness at not being with Christ yet, while at the same time offering him hope and encouragement that he will one day be in his presence. The image of exile both illuminates and shapes his thoughts at this point:

All this I hold with unwavering faith,
  and weep over the hardship of exile,
hoping in the sole consolation of your coming,
ardently longing for the glorious contemplation of your face.

On the basis of this map of life, medieval spiritual writers began to develop a series of insights that illuminated the status of Christians and offered them guidance as to how they should behave in the world. For example, they stressed the importance of cultivating the hope of return to the homeland. Many writers of the period offered powerful visual images of the heavenly Jerusalem in order to encourage their readers to set their hearts firmly on heaven. The Old Testament indicates that some exiled inhabitants of Jerusalem actually came to prefer Babylon and chose to stay on in that city when others returned home. Bernard of Clairvaux (c. 1090–1153) and others discerned a similar danger in the Christian life – that Christians will come to prefer their place of exile to their homeland and in effect will choose to remain in exile. Yet the dominant theme is that of hope – resting assured that our future homeland exists and that we shall finally enter there.

We are in exile and dream of our homeland. Like Gregory Petrov, we are able to contemplate the hope of entering that homeland, even while in a labour camp. There are signs around us to reassure us of this hope and to encourage us to anticipate that future joy.

12 THE MOTH AND THE STAR

We began this book by reflecting on the deep sense of wonder evoked within us by the sight of the night sky. The brilliance of the stars has always been able to unlock some of the heart's deepest fears and hopes, bringing to light the hidden longings that are part of our human condition. So what might these feelings mean? Do they mean anything at all?

Literature often opens doors of perception, allowing us to crystallize our thinking about such complex issues. The English poet Percy Bysshe Shelley (1792–1822) saw the moth's desire for the star as a powerful symbol of the heart's desire for something which was both distant yet compelling, a means of sustaining hope for the future and distracting us from our present 'sphere of sorrow'. It is a poignant image, which can help us reflect on the theme of meaning.

The moth is meant to be attracted to the light. For some reason that we do not fully understand, the moth has an inbuilt tendency to be drawn to a light source. Why? We can but guess. Yet, despite all our guesses and theories, the simple fact remains that moths are drawn to the light. It is as if they have an innate tendency to be attracted to a source of illumination.

With the arrival of artificial light, the moth has found itself in something of a difficulty. The candle lit at night attracts moths, who end up being consumed in its flame. The floodlit buildings in the centre of our cities attract moths to the powerful lights that illuminate them – and which vaporize the moths on contact. The inbuilt attraction of the moth for the wrong light source thus leads to its destruction.

Is there not a parallel here with our own situation? Suppose that the deep sense of yearning for something that really satisfies us is actually a longing for God – a longing that we are meant to experience, and a longing that is meant to lead us to its true source and goal in God. Might not this longing accidentally become attached to lesser goals within this world? Might our quest for beauty become an end in itself, yet break our hearts because it fails to deliver what we had anticipated? Might our quest for significance end up being completely frustrated in that everything that we hoped would bring meaning to our lives seems to disappoint us? The objects of our desire have a marked tendency to let us down. But suppose that these objects are like the candle to the moth – something which is only an image of our true desire? Might there be something, which is what we really are meant to desire, that will not destroy us but bring us fulfilment and joy?

This is the essence of the Christian hope. We have been made to relate to God, and our true joy lies in the fulfilment of that God-given potential. It is not something that we are required to achieve or fulfil on our own. It may seem to us that we are engaged on a quest for meaning and truth; in fact, the truth is engaged on a quest for us and has drawn close to us. The God who created us has entered into our history and drawn close to us, whispering our names in the night and waiting and longing for us to respond to him. The God who longs to fulfil us awaits us, inviting us to open the door of our lives so that he may enter in.

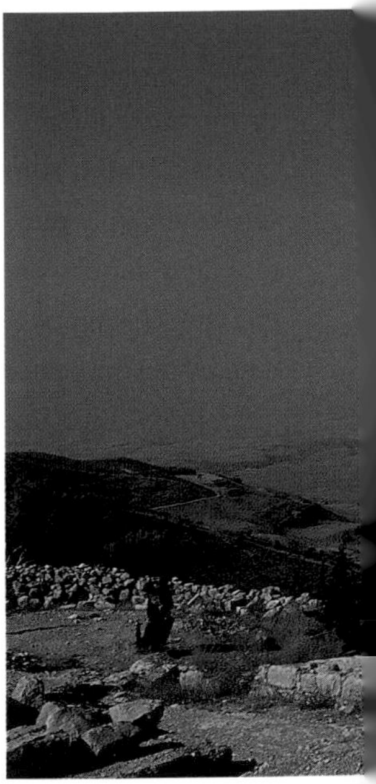

How can such hope be sustained? How can we be assured that this is a real hope, and not simply some soporific to dull us to a harsher reality that is just too painful to bear? In the end, we cannot be absolutely sure. Nobody can be totally certain about this, one way or the other. It is all a matter of trust. All the clues are there – but they are not decisive. In the end, we have to trust our hearts, as much as our minds, to aid us in reaching a decision. 'The heart has its reasons, which the mind does not know about' (Blaise Pascal).

So is this a blind leap of faith – a random decision, without any basis in reality? In the end, the decision is going to rest upon trust. Imagine the people of Israel at another period in their history – the time of the exodus from Egypt, perhaps dating from 14 centuries before Christ. Israel left their bondage in Egypt behind. But what lay ahead? The answer was clear: there was 'a land flowing with milk and honey' (Exodus 3:8) ahead, beyond the wilderness they had now entered. Not one of those Israelites had ever seen that land. Not even Moses had ever seen that land. There was no way of confirming its existence, or verifying that it was indeed fertile and verdant. The decision to go onwards rested on trust. But was there a promised land? Or was it just a dream of a people without a land and hence without hope?

It was only when the people of Israel crossed the River Jordan that those doubts were resolved. Moses himself never got to enter that land; he died while still on the far side of the Jordan. Yet before he died, he was able to climb Mount Nebo and look over the Jordan to the land that lay beyond – the land which had dominated his thoughts and hopes since Israel had left

LOOKING ACROSS THE JORDAN VALLEY FROM MOUNT NEBO TOWARDS ISRAEL

behind the captivity of Egypt. Perhaps the land was shimmering in the sunlight, or shrouded in mist. We shall never know. Yet Moses was able to die, knowing that his life's goal lay to hand.

What of us? We can look to the past for guidance. Might not the experience of Israel help us to trust and hence to journey in hope? We can look to our own experience, and that of countless others, knowing in our hearts that our sense of longing is a God-given clue to our destiny, a 'yearning for the happiness that will last for ever in the eternal native land' (Gregory Petrov). We can look to the person of Jesus Christ, seen by Christians as the ground and guarantor of trust in God, and as the ultimate ground for trusting that there is indeed a homeland awaiting us – where countless others await us, having trusted and journeyed in the past.

We cannot know for certain; we can, however, trust. In the end, every worldview rests upon trust, in that none can be conclusively demonstrated to be true – atheism included. Our choice will rest upon probability, rather than certainty; our hearts, as well as our minds. Yet this is nothing new. It has always been so. Our decision must rest on our assessment of what is the best explanation of the puzzle of existence.

In this book, we have explored one approach. It is an approach with a long and distinguished history, which countless people have found meaningful, even compelling, down the ages. In common with its rivals, it cannot be proved. Yet it offers a deep appeal to both the heart and the mind. In bringing this book to a close, we may try to set out its leading themes, using analogies drawn from the classic tradition and from the New Testament.

Our first image is of Plato's cave – the dark world of flickering shadows, in which a group of people are held captive. Yet in their hearts, they may have known that there is a better world. Clues within the cave pointed to something lying beyond it, a world of which they could only dream and hope. But what if someone were to come to them from the world beyond that cave and speak to them of its colours, sounds and fragrances? And more than this: what if this visitor were to lead them from the cramped

and gloomy cave to a brilliant and spacious world beyond, in which a vast expanse of verdant meadows lay ahead of them on a bright sunlit spring afternoon, with blue-tinged mountains shimmering in the distance? That is the essence of the tale that we have told – of a God who enters into our situation in order to tell us of another kingdom and lead us into its safety and joy.

Or we could reflect on the image of the shepherd seeking his lost sheep (Luke 15:3–7). The sheep may have a memory of its home but cannot find its way back. Yet the shepherd entered into the domain of its lostness, seeking it out – and having found it, carried it home with him. The shepherd provides both the goal and the means to that goal. In the same way, Christ enters our fallen and frail world, determined to find us and bring us to where our true destiny lies. He has already gone there ahead of us, to prepare a

place for us. And already our hearts feel the pull of that realm, as we long to be there and anticipate the return to that homeland.

How can this be proved? It cannot – but neither can its alternatives. Yet that nagging deep sense of longing remains within us, unexplained – a longing that we know cannot be satisfied by anything within this world. Might this be like the desire of the moth for the star – a longing for something that, though distant, is compelling? As we wander in the night, might the distant stars whisper clues to our true destiny? Might they be pointing to something that lies beyond them? Could we reach out and touch the face of God?

Something lies beyond the horizon of our experience and beckons us onwards to discover it – and, by doing so, to enter into the greatest discovery that life can offer. The great Scottish preacher Horatius Bonar (1808–89) summed up our situation rather well, and it is fitting to end with his words:

We are but as wayfarers, wandering in the lonely night, who see dimly upon the distant mountain peak the reflection of a sun that never rises here, but which shall never set in the 'new heavens' thereafter. And this is enough. It comforts and cheers us on our dark and rugged way.

Picture Acknowledgments

The Bridgeman Art Library, London: pp. 12 (portrait of Karl Marx [1818–93] [photo], private collection), 15 (Sherlock Holmes, cartoon from *Vanity Fair* of the actor William Gillette, private collection), 32 (Charles Darwin [1809–82] [photo] by Julia Margaret Cameron [1815–79], private collection/the Stapleton Collection), 47 (Sir Christopher Wren [1632–1723], engraved by James Godby [fl. 1790–1820], published by Edward Orme, 1815, after Giovanni Battista Cipriani [1727–85], City of Westminster Archive Centre, London, UK), 62–63 (*St Paul Preaching at Athens* [cartoon for the Sistine Chapel, pre-restoration] by Raphael [Raffaello Sanzio of Urbino] [1483–1520], Victoria & Albert Museum, London, UK), 67 (*The Sermon on the Mount*, illustration for *The Life of Christ*, c. 1886–96 [gouache on paperboard] by James Jacques Joseph Tissot [1836–1902], Brooklyn Museum of Art, New York, USA), 73 (*The Incredulity of St Thomas*, 1602–1603 [oil on canvas] by Michelangelo Merisi da Caravaggio [1571–1610)], Schloss Sanssouci, Potsdam, Germany), 79 (*Master Isaac Newton*, 1905 [oil on canvas] by Robert Hannah [1812–1909], The Royal Institution, London, UK), 83 (*St Augustine in His Cell* [fresco] by Sandro Botticelli [1444/5–1510], Ognissanti, Florence, Italy).

Corbis Stock Market: p. 121 (flowers in fog and Mount Rainier from Paradise Park, Washington, USA, copyright © 1999 Craig Tuttle/Corbis Stock Market).

Hulton Archive: pp. 36–37 (May Day Parade in Moscow, 8 May 1952, copyright © Hulton Getty).

Hutchison Picture Library: pp. 94–95 (hillside cross, Seychelles, copyright © Patricio Goycolea/Hutchison Picture Library).

Hanan Isachar: pp. 118–19 (copyright © Hanan Isachar).

Jon Arnold Images: pp. 60–61 (Athens), 114–15 (Jerusalem).

Lion Publishing/David Townsend: pp. 122–23.

The National Gallery, London: p. 105 (*The Trinity* by Jacopo di Cione [active 1362, died 1398/1400]).

Oxford Scientific Films: pp. 7 (halo of neutrinos around the Milky Way galaxy, copyright © NASA), 26 (dawn reflection, Los Glaciares, Patagonian Andes, Argentina, copyright © Colin Monteath/Hedgehog House), 28–29 (Neptune from *Voyager 2*, copyright © NASA), 42–43 (light house, Nugget Point, New Zealand, copyright © Colin Monteath), 52–53 (Moraine Lake, Banff National Park, Alberta, Canada, copyright © Adam Jones), 70–71 (sea-gold fish in the Red Sea, copyright © Laurence Gould).

Nicholas Rous: pp. 16–17, 20–21, 110–11.

Science Photo Library: pp. 38 (water-drop impact, copyright © Adam Hart-Davis), 56 (starfield over Bonilla Point, Vancouver Island, Canada, during June, copyright © David Nunuk), 80 (portrait of Galileo Galilei [1564–1642]), 92 (portrait of Albert Einstein [1879–1955] [photo] by Orren Turner, copyright © US Library of Congress).

SuperStock Ltd: pp. 10 (Socrates [marble bust], Museo Capitolino, Rome, Italy), 49 (St Paul's Cathedral, London, UK), 74 (*Nativity with Music-Making Angels Above* by Giovanni Battista [1497–1555], Christie's Images), 90 (*Adam and Eve* by Lucas Cranach the Elder [1472–1553], German private collection), 99, 100–101 (Death Valley, California, USA).